LONELY LIVES

A DRAMA

By GERHART HAUPTMANN

Translated from the German by

MARY MORISON

LONDON: WILLIAM HEINEMANN

MDCCCXCVIII

CHARACTERS

VOCKERAT

MRS. VOCKERAT

JOHN VOCKERAT

KITTY VOCKERAT, *John's Wife*

BRAUN

MISS ANNA MAHR

PASTOR KOLLIN

MRS. LEHMANN

SERVANTS

The action of the play passes at Friedrichshagen, near Berlin, in a country house with a garden stretching down to a little lake, the Müggelsee.

The scene of all five acts is the same.

A large room, comfortably furnished to serve both as dining and sitting-room. Cottage piano; bookcase, at both sides of which hang photographs and engravings of modern men of science (including theologians), among them Haeckel and Darwin. Above the piano, portrait of a pastor in gown and bands. The other pictures are reproductions of sacred subjects by Schnorr von Carolsfeld.

One door in the left wall, two in the right. The door on the left leads into JOHN VOCKERAT'S *study. One of those on the right leads into a bedroom, the other into the entrance-hall.*

At the back two bow windows and a glass door look on to a verandah, the garden, lake, and the Müggel Hills beyond.

Time : The present day.

LONELY LIVES

THE FIRST ACT

*The stage is empty. From the study, the door of which
is ajar, comes the sound of a pastor's voice raised
in exhortation. After a few seconds it stops. Then
the chords of a chorale, played on a harmonium,
are heard.*

*During the first bars the door is thrown open. Enter
MRS. VOCKERAT, SEN., KITTY VOCKERAT, and the
NURSE with a baby in long-clothes. All in gala
attire.*

MRS. VOCKERAT : *Matronly appearance ; between fifty
and sixty. Black silk dress. False front.* KITTY :
*twenty-one ; middle height, slightly built, pale,
brunette, gentle in manner. Advanced stage of
convalescence.*

MRS. VOCKERAT.

[*Takes her daughter-in-law's hand, and caresses it.*]
Well, Kitty, was it not beautiful, what he said ?

> [KITTY *smiles constrainedly, nods mechanic-
> ally, and turns towards the child.*

A

NURSE.

The sweet little man! There, there! [*She rocks him in her arms.*] He's going to sleep now, though, he is—sh! sh! sh! nothing more to say to any one, he hasn't. [*She removes a ribbon that is annoying the child.*] There, there!—hm! hm! hm! Sleep, ducky, sleep. [*Hums with closed lips the tune of "Sleep, baby, sleep!"*] But what a saucy face the little man made at the Pastor—like this! [*Imitates it.*] Ha! ha! till the water came, ha! ha! That was too much for him. [*She sings.*] "Hush-a-by, baby, on the tree top!" Ha! ha! what a roar he gave then—ow, ow, ow, ow! Sleep, baby, sleep. . . . [*Beats time with her foot.*]

[KITTY *laughs rather hysterically.*

MRS. VOCKERAT.

Just look, Kitty! how sweet! What beautiful long eyelashes the little fellow has!

NURSE.

Ha, ha! he got these from his mammy. Sleep, baby. . . . Reg'lar fringes they are.

MRS. VOCKERAT.

It's true, Kitty—he's his mother all over!

[KITTY *shakes her head energetically in deprecation.*

MRS. VOCKERAT.

He really is, though.

KITTY.

[*Speaking with an effort.*] But, mother dear—that's not what I want at all. He's *not* to be like me. I— [*She gets no farther.*]

MRS. VOCKERAT.

[*Tries to change the subject.*] He's a fine strong child.

NURSE.

A splendid fellow.

MRS. VOCKERAT.

Look at these fists, Kitty.

NURSE.

Fists like—like a Goliath.

KITTY.

[*Kisses the child.*] He has a beautiful broad chest, mother, has he not?

NURSE.

I'll answer for that, ma'am—it's like a general's. Sh! sh! He'll be a match for any five some day.

MRS. VOCKERAT.

Come, come now, nurse. [*She and* KITTY *laugh.*]

NURSE.

And it's good sound blood he has too, sh! sh! And the blood's the life, you know, sh! sh! [*Half singing.*] Hush-a-by! Come along—come along! We're go—ing, go—ing to by—bye: sh! sh! sh! Sleep, baby . . . [*Exit into bedroom.*

MRS. VOCKERAT.

[*Closes the door behind the* NURSE, *and turns round, shaking her head and laughing.*] What a woman that is! But she's a first-rate nurse, Kitty. I'm glad you have been so lucky.

KITTY.

A general—well, well! [*She laughs. The laugh becomes hysterical, and threatens to end in tears.*]

MRS. VOCKERAT.

[*Alarmed.*]   Kitty!—Kitty!

[KITTY *controls herself.*

MRS. VOCKERAT.

[*With her arms round* KITTY.]   My little Kate!

KITTY.

There is—nothing—the matter with me.

MRS. VOCKERAT.

But I'm sure there is! And no wonder, for you have not got back your strength yet. Come and lie down for a few minutes.

KITTY.

I'm—I'm quite well now, mother.

MRS. VOCKERAT.

But you'll lie down for a little all the same.

KITTY.

Oh no—please not! Besides, it is just dinner-time.

MRS. VOCKERAT.

[*At the table, on which stand cake and wine, pouring out a glass of wine.*] There, anyhow swallow a mouthful of that. Take a sip! It's nice and sweet.

[KITTY *drinks.*

MRS. VOCKERAT.

That puts a little strength into you, does it not? What ever were you thinking of, my dear child? You must still be very careful—that's all—and take things as they come! and don't worry yourself!—It will all come right. Now that baby has come, everything will be different. John will quiet down again. . . .

KITTY.

Oh, mother, if he only would!

MRS. VOCKERAT.

Think of his delight when the boy was born! He has always been crazy about children. You may be quite sure of it. It's always the way. A marriage without children isn't half a marriage—it's nothing at all. How I have prayed God to bless you two with a child! When I think how it was with ourselves. . . . We dragged through four years, papa and I, but what sort of a life was it! Then God heard our prayers and sent us John. And it was not till then, Kitty, that we really began to live! Only wait till the first three months are over, and you'll see what a joy your child will be to you. Yes, yes, Kitty! you are a lucky woman; you have your boy, you have a husband who loves you, there is enough for you all to live on; what more would you have?

KITTY.

I daresay it is foolish. Yes, I am sure it is. I really do often worry unnecessarily.

MRS. VOCKERAT.

You must not be angry with me, Kitty, but—but you would find far more peace, far more—if . . . . When things are troubling me very badly, and I pray, pray earnestly, cast all my care on our dear Father in heaven, my burden is lightened, I feel glad at heart. . . . No, no! the learned men may say what they like for me—there is a God, Kitty!—a faithful Father in heaven; you may be sure of that. A man

without religion is bad enough; but a woman without
religion. . . . Don't be angry with me, Kitty.
That's all! That's all! I'll say no more about it.
I have prayed so much. I pray every day : and God
will answer my prayers; I know He will. Dear,
good people you both are, already. He will make you
His own believing children. [*She kisses her daughter.
The chorale is at an end.*] Dear, dear! I'm forgetting
myself.

KITTY.

If I were only a little stronger, mammy dear! I
can't bear sitting idle and seeing you toiling away.

MRS. VOCKERAT.

[*At door into hall.*] How can you talk such nonsense? It's holiday time here. When you are quite
well again, I'll sit still and you shall work for me.

[*Exit.*

[*As* KITTY *is going towards the bedroom,*
BRAUN *enters from the study, where the
baptism has taken place.*

BRAUN, *aged twenty-six ; pale face ; wearied expression ; hollow-eyed ; slight ; downy moustache ;
hair very closely cropped ; dress, in the fashion,
but verging on the shabby-genteel. He is phleg-
matic, generally dissatisfied, and consequently ill-
humoured.*

BRAUN.

Well! [*Standing, takes a cigarette from his case.*]
That's over, anyhow!

KITTY.

And very well you stood it, Mr. Braun.

BRAUN.

[*Lights his cigarette.*] I should have been better
employed—painting. Goodness gracious! What a
hullabaloo to make for nothing !

KITTY.

I daresay you'll manage to make up for lost time.

BRAUN.

Yes. We're a lazy lot. I know it well. [*Sits down
at the table.*] After all, there *is* something about a
baptism !

KITTY.

Did you notice John ?

BRAUN.

[*Quickly.*] Extraordinarily restless, you mean! I
was afraid the whole time that something would
happen ; once thought he was actually going to break
in on the Pastor's address. But can you imagine any
sane man talking such stuff ?

KITTY.

Oh, Mr. Braun !

BRAUN.

You know it was, Mrs. John ! Except for that, no
complaints to make. I may paint a scene of the kind
some day. Rare good subject !

KITTY.

Are you in earnest, Mr. Braun ?

BRAUN.

That picture, when it is painted, will exhale a
perfume of olden days—a sort of mixture, you know,
of Rhine wine, cake, snuff, and wax candles ; a sort

of. . . . It will produce a pleasing, swimmy feeling,
a kind of youthful intoxication. . . .

> [*Enter* JOHN VOCKERAT *from the study :
> twenty-eight ; middle height ; fair, intel-
> lectual face ; expressive play of feature ;
> restless in all his movements ; faultlessly
> dressed—frock-coat, white tie and gloves.
> He sighs, takes off his gloves.*

BRAUN.

Well—had your feelings finely touched up?

JOHN.

Can't say I have.   What about dinner, Kitty?

KITTY.

[*Hesitatingly.*] I thought we might have it out on
the verandah.

JOHN.

What do you mean ?   Is it laid out there ?

KITTY.

[*Timidly.*] Would you rather not ?   I thought. . . .

JOHN.

Kitty, for goodness' sake, don't go on as if you were
frightened !   As if I were going to eat you up.   I
can't stand it.

KITTY.

[*Compelling herself to speak firmly.*]   I have had it
laid out on the verandah.

JOHN.

All right !   Of course !   Very nice out there !
As if I were an ogre !

BRAUN.

[*Mutters.*] Oh, stop that nagging!

JOHN.

[*Putting his arm round* KITTY, *good-humouredly.*] It's quite true, Kitty. You go on as if I were a regular tyrant. A second Uncle Peter, or something in that line. You must really try to get out of the habit.

KITTY.

But you *are* sometimes angry about things John. . . .

JOHN.

And what if I am? That's no misfortune. Just you give it me back again! Stand up for yourself! I can't help my nature. Don't let yourself be trampled on. I know nothing so utterly objectionable as your patient, Madonna-like person. . . .

KITTY.

There now, Jack! Don't excite yourself for nothing. It's not worth talking about.

JOHN.

[*Excitedly.*] Oh, oh, oh! There you're very far wrong. I'm not excited at all, not in the very least. It's extraordinary the way I am supposed always to get excited. [BRAUN *is going to speak.*] All right then! You all know better than I do. Good! We'll change the subject. . . . [*Sighs*]. Well, well, well!!

BRAUN.

It grows tiresome in time, that eternal sigh, sighing.

JOHN.

[*Puts his hand to his breast, his face twitches with pain.*] Oh, oh !

BRAUN.

What now ?

JOHN.

Nothing !   Only the old story—these pains in my chest—like stabs they are.

BRAUN.

Stab back again, Jack.

JOHN.

That's all very well, my boy, but it's no laughing matter.   Oh, oh . . . !

KITTY.

You must not be nervous about it, Jack dear.   It's nothing serious.

JOHN.

You forget that I have twice had inflammation of the lungs.

BRAUN.

And that man calls himself a soldier—sets up to be an officer of the reserve !

JOHN.

What can I take for it ?

BRAUN.

Old hypochondriac !   Stop that nonsense !   Have something to eat !   It's the sermon that is sticking in your throat.

JOHN.

To tell the truth, Braun . . . the way you speak of

baptism. . . . You know the light in which I look upon it. Certainly not from the Christian point of view. Yet it is a thing still held sacred by so many.

BRAUN.

But not by me.

JOHN.

I know that. Nor by me personally. Just as little as by you. But you have surely some small degree of reverence left for a ceremony, which for so . . .

BRAUN.

Bother you and your reverence !

JOHN.

I just wish you had a little of it.

BRAUN.

Yes, you would like one to have reverence for the very sticks and stones that trip one up on the road. Sheer sentimentality !

JOHN.

Excuse me, Braun, but I. . . . Perhaps another time I'll be able to take it from you better than to-day.

[*Exit on to the verandah, where he is seen doing Swedish gymnastic exercises.*

[BRAUN *rises, looks embarrassed, laughs pointlessly.*

KITTY.

[*Standing at her work-table.*] You have hurt him, Mr. Braun.

BRAUN.

[*With an embarrassed laugh, brusquely.*] It can't be helped. I have a deadly hatred of all compromise.

KITTY.

[*After a pause.*] You misjudge him.

BRAUN.

In what way ?

KITTY.

I can't tell you. . . . I am not able to express myself. But anyhow . . . John is honest.

BRAUN.

When did he begin to be so dreadfully irritable again, I should like to know ?

KITTY.

He has been so ever since we had to arrange about the baptism. I was beginning to be so happy. . . . then that unsettled him again altogether. And yet it's nothing but a form. Were we for the sake of that to make his old parents utterly miserable ? . . . no, certainly not. Just think of them—these pious, strictly orthodox people. You must see yourself that it could not be helped, Mr. Braun.

JOHN.

[*Opens the glass-door and calls in.*] Good people, I was rather ill-tempered. Cheer up ! We're all right again.   [*Exit into garden.*

BRAUN.

Ass !

[*Pause.*

KITTY.

He is really touching sometimes, poor John !

[*Pause.*

[*Enter old* VOCKERAT *and* PASTOR KOLLIN *noisily from the study.* VOCKERAT *is*

*upwards of sixty. Grey hair, red beard,
freckled face and hands. Strong and
broad-shouldered, inclining to stoutness.
He has begun to stoop and walks with
short steps. Overflowing with affection
and friendliness. Cheerful, simple, opti-
mistic temperament.* PASTOR KOLLIN, *old
man of seventy-three; wears a skull-cap
and takes snuff.*

VOCKERAT.

[*Leading in the* PASTOR *by the hand, speaking in a
soft, slightly husky voice.*] Many, many thanks, my
dear sir! Our best thanks for your beautiful words.
They were real refreshment to my soul, yes, yes!
And here's my dear little daughter! [*Goes up to*
KITTY, *embraces and kisses her heartily.*] My dear,
dear Kitty! My very heartiest good wishes! [*Kiss.*]
Once more, in his great goodness, God has, yes . . .
has, in his never-ending goodness revealed himself to
us. [*Kiss.*] His mercy and goodness are boundless.
Now he will, yes . . . he will now have the little one
too in his fatherly, yes—fatherly keeping, yes, yes!
[*To* BRAUN.] Allow me, Mr. Braun, to shake hands
with you too. [*Re-enter* JOHN; VOCKERAT *goes to meet
him.*] And here is my dear boy John! [*Kiss. Hearty
embrace. Half-laughing from excess of emotion.*] I
am happy in your happiness. I am truly happy. I
can't be grateful enough to God, yes, yes!

PASTOR KOLLIN.

[*Trembles a little, short-winded; shakes hands solemnly
with* KITTY.] Once more God's richest blessing!
[*Shakes hand with* JOHN.] God's richest blessing!

VOCKERAT.

And now, my dear sir, may we offer you something?
—What! you won't take anything?

JOHN.

At least a glass of wine, sir. I'll fetch a fresh bottle
this moment.

PASTOR KOLLIN.

Don't put yourself to any trouble on my account; I
beg of you, don't.

JOHN.

May I give you port or . . .

PASTOR KOLLIN.

Quite the same to me, quite the same. But—I beg
of you—entreat you !—not to take any trouble on my
account. [*Exit* JOHN.] I must be . . .

> [*He looks for his hat, overcoat, and long
> muffler, which are on a rack beside the
> door.*

VOCKERAT.

You are not going already, Mr. Kollin?

PASTOR KOLLIN.

I must indeed, Mr. Vockerat! My sermon, you
know. Who is there to preach for me to-morrow?

> [BRAUN *holds the* PASTOR'S *overcoat ready for
> him.*

PASTOR KOLLIN.

[*Putting his arms into the sleeves.*] Thanks to you,
young man!

KITTY.

Would you not do us the honour, Mr. Kollin, to
take a plain dinner with us?

PASTOR KOLLIN.

[*Busy with his muffler.*] Very kind of you—very kind, Mrs. Vockerat! But . . .

VOCKERAT.

My dear Pastor, you must really give us that pleasure.

PASTOR KOLLIN.

[*Hesitating.*] But you know—you know . . .

VOCKERAT.

If we all ask it as a great favour.

PASTOR KOLLIN.

And what about that holy word of God, eh, that I am to preach to-morrow? Eh! preach, you know—to-morrow—God's word.

> [JOHN *has come in again, and pours out some glasses of wine.*

VOCKERAT.

[*Takes a glass; tastes it before presenting.*] In the meantime . . . you won't refuse us the pleasure of drinking a glass of wine with us.

PASTOR KOLLIN.

[*Takes the glass from* VOCKERAT.] No—I couldn't do that—you know. Well, here is to the health . . . to the health of the dear child! [*They all touch glasses.*] May he be a good, true child of God all his life long!

VOCKERAT.

[*Quietly.*] God grant it!

JOHN.

[*Offering the* PASTOR *a cigar.*] You smoke, sir, don't you?

PASTOR KOLLIN.

Thanks, I do! [*Takes a cigar, cuts off the end.*]
Thanks! [*Lights his cigar at* JOHN's.] Pf! pf! [*Has
great difficulty in getting it to draw. At last it burns.
Looks round.*] What a pretty room this is, pf, pf—
such good taste, you know! [*He first glances generally
at the pictures, then examines them more closely. Stops
before an engraving representing Jacob wrestling with
the Angel.*] I—will not let—thee go—pf, pf! except
thou bless me.

[*Mutters to himself in a satisfied tone.*]

KITTY.

[*A little uneasy.*] Papa dear, don't you think . . .
it's so pleasant out in the garden now. Ever so much
warmer than it is indoors. Perhaps you and Mr.
Kollin would like . . . I can easily have the tray
carried out.

PASTOR KOLLIN.

[*Has arrived at the portraits of the scientists beside
the bookcase.*] A mixed company! I suppose these
are—pf, pf!—your old professors, Dr. Vockerat?
Well, well!

JOHN.

[*Slightly embarrassed.*] Yes, sir, they are . . . that
is . . . of course, with the exception of Darwin.

PASTOR KOLLIN.

[*Peering closely at the pictures.*] Darwin? Darwin?
I see—Darwin! Yes, yes! hm! Well, you know!
[*He spells out.*] Ernst—Haeckel. Autograph, too, no
less! Pf, pf! [*With a touch of irony.*] And so *he*
was one of your teachers?

JOHN.

[*Quickly and rather fierily.*] Yes, and I am proud
of it, Mr. Kollin. . . .

VOCKERAT.

My daughter is right, Mr. Kollin. It is much
warmer out of doors. If it is all the same to you, I'll
carry out the wine and our glasses.

PASTOR KOLLIN.

Certainly!—pf, pf !—of course, of course!—pf, pf !—
but only for a few minutes, you know—only for a few
minutes ! [*Going out with* VOCKERAT, *a little hurt.*]
Man, Mr. Vockerat, man is, you know—pf, pf !—no
longer God's image, you know. The monkey, you
know—pf, pf !—according to the conclusions of natural
science, I mean . . .

[*Exit on to the verandah, from which both gen-
tlemen, gesticulating animatedly, descend
into the garden.* BRAUN *laughs to himself.*

JOHN.

What are you laughing at ?

BRAUN.

What, I ? Because I am pleased.

JOHN.

You are pleased?

BRAUN.

Yes. Any reason why I should not be ?

JOHN.

None at all! none at all! [*He walks up and
down, sighs, and suddenly says to* KITTY, *who is in*

the act of leaving the room.] I say, I'm afraid I expressed myself rather strongly.

KITTY.

I think you did—rather.

JOHN.

[*Shrugging his shoulders.*] Well, good people all! it's their own fault. I can't stand it. There's a limit to everything. If they will provoke me . . .

KITTY.

Oh, it was nothing very bad !

JOHN.

Was it not ?

KITTY.

I shouldn't wonder if he never noticed it.

JOHN.

[*Walking about, scratching his head.*] Still, it makes me feel uncomfortable.

BRAUN.

Well, it's always something for you to be cross about, Jack.

JOHN.

[*Suddenly furious.*] The devil !—can't they let me alone ? They had better not carry it too far, or— once my patience gives way . . .

BRAUN.

Don't get into a rage !

JOHN.

[*Turning on* BRAUN.] As for you, it's nothing but brag. Idea-braggarts, that's what you and your

friends are—nothing more! What good can it do
me to tell the old man the truth, I should like to
know? When you begin like that, Braun, you cure
me of my ill-humour at once. I see instantly how
perfectly childish it is of me to let such people cause
me annoyance. It is as if I were to be annoyed
because pines bear needles and not leaves. One must
be objective, my boy.

BRAUN.

In science, perhaps, but not in life.

JOHN.

Friends, friends! The whole thing is hateful to
me! . . . hateful! . . . you don't know how hateful! [*Stamps about the stage.*

BRAUN.

[*Walking from the stove, by which he has been standing, to the table, and putting the stump of his cigar
into the ash-tray.*] And do you suppose it's not
equally so to me? And often enough too! But to
be perpetually moaning and groaning because of it—
I'll be hanged if that's the way to take it!

JOHN.

[*Mood changed, laughing.*] Come, come! for
Heaven's sake don't excite yourself. There is no
question of perpetual moaning and groaning. An
occasional sigh does no harm. It's a gasp for air,
nothing worse than that. No, no—my view of life is
by no means so dark as yours; I'm not nearly so far
on the road to bankruptcy as you are.

BRAUN.

Quite possible.

JOHN.

Are you pretending that you are a model character?

BRAUN.

Not in the very least.

JOHN.

Oh, bankrupt, bankrupt! what *is* being bankrupt? You are no more bankrupt than I am. I just wish now that I had not spoiled the Governor's and the Pastor's pleasure.

KITTY.

[*Embracing* JOHN.] Dear old Jack! Cheer up, cheer up!

JOHN.

And my work is weighing on my mind, too. It's a fortnight again since I have been able to touch it.

BRAUN.

You are a coward! You don't acknowledge to yourself what a poor thing it is to . . .

JOHN.

[*Who has not heard.*] What?

BRAUN.

It's wet when it rains, it's white when it snows, there's wind when it blows.

JOHN.

Ass

KITTY.

Cheer up, Jack! Think of our little Philip! We'll shut ourselves up here, and all be so comfortable together this winter. You'll see how well the work will get on then.

JOHN.

I have finished the fourth chapter, Breo, do you know ?

BRAUN.

[*Carelessly.*] Have you ?

JOHN.

Look at this manuscript ! The mere list of authorities quoted takes up twelve pages. That means work, eh ? I promise you there will be head-shaking over this.

BRAUN.

No doubt.

JOHN.

Here, for instance, [*He turns over the leaves of his manuscript*] here I attack Dubois-Reymond.

BRAUN.

I say, Jack, don't read it to me just now. I'm in such a beastly bad humour . . . some other time.

JOHN.

[*Resignedly.*] No, no! of course not ! I never meant to. I . . .

KITTY.

Besides, dinner is just ready.

JOHN.

No, of course not ! I never even thought of it ; I was only—oh, dear, dear ! [*Sighing, he puts the manuscript back into the bookcase.*]

KITTY.

Cheer up, Jack ! cheer up !

JOHN.

I'm perfectly cheerful, Kitty.

KITTY.

No, Jack; you were, but you're not now.

JOHN.

If only one person in the wide world cared about me at all ! It's not much I ask for. The least little bit of appreciation, the least little scrap of understanding of my work.

KITTY.

Now, you are to be reasonable, Jack, and not go plaguing yourself, but have patience. You'll see the time will come when they will acknowledge . . .

JOHN.

But in the meantime ? Do you imagine that it's easy ? with no support at all ? . . . Do you think a man's able to stand that indefinitely ?

KITTY.

Yes, I do. Come, Jack, when your thoughts are too much for you, the only thing is to get away from them. Come and look at little Philip. He's so sweet when he's asleep. He always lies like this [*Imitating the position of his arms*], clenching his little fists. He's too funny. Come along !

JOHN.

[*To* BRAUN.] Won't you come too ?

BRAUN.

Not I, Jack; I take no stock in babies. I'm going for a turn in the garden.   [*Exit by verandah.*

JOHN.

A queer fellow, that.

KITTY.

[*Opens the bedroom door cautiously.*] You've no idea how perfectly sweet he is! Hush—h! quiet! quite quiet. . . . [*Exit both, on tiptoe, and hand in hand.*

MRS. VOCKERAT *and a* MAID *have been occupied laying the table on the verandah. Now a loud sound is heard of crockery falling and smashing. A sudden short scream, and the* MAID *rushes through the room—from verandah towards entrance-hall.* MRS. VOCKERAT *follows, scolding.*

MRS. VOCKERAT.

This is really too much of a good thing, Minna! Never a day but you break something! And that beautiful mayonnaise! [*Exit* MAID.] Such a thing would never happen in my house. I'd teach these maids a lesson!

JOHN.

[*Hearing the noise, comes from the bedroom.*] What's the matter, mother? [*Puts his arm round her, soothingly.*] Quiet, quiet now! Mustn't excite yourself, mammy.

KITTY.

[*Opening the door a little.*] What ever was it?

JOHN.

Nothing! nothing at all.

[KITTY *draws back her head.*

MRS. VOCKERAT.

Just listen to him! Nothing at all, indeed! She

has broken good ten shillings worth of dishes.
Nothing at all!   And all that beautiful mayonnaise!
Well. . . .   [*Pushes* JOHN *away.*

JOHN.

Mammy, mammy! we'll do very well without the
mayonnaise.

MRS. VOCKERAT.

No, no, Jack.   You and Kitty don't take matters
seriously enough.   You forget that you can't afford to
waste things.   You're far too easy with the girls.   It
only makes them uppish.

JOHN.

Well, but, if they're always handling the dishes. . . .

MRS. VOCKERAT.

I'm not a tyrant.   I keep my servants six, seven
years.   But what they break they pay for.   Of course
in *your* house they're fed on cream-tarts and caviare!
No, no!   These are your fine new ideas; but they
don't go down with me—they don't.

JOHN.

[*Cheerfully.*] Come, now, mammy, don't be cross.

MRS. VOCKERAT.

I'm not a bit cross, boy. [*Kisses him.*] But you're
a hare-brained fellow all the same.   You're not fit for
this world.

[*The* MAID *is seen on the verandah, cleaning
up, and lifting the broken china.*

JOHN.

[*With a slight start.*] Is that what you think,
mother? [*Jocosely.*] But what a face you're making,

mammy . . . Why are you looking like that—so
frightened—so anxious ?

MRS. VOCKERAT.

I, John ? What do you mean ? What sort of face
am I making ? I don't know what you're talking
about !

JOHN.

Look at me again.

MRS. VOCKERAT.

You silly fellow ! *[Looks fixedly at him.*

JOHN.

That's all right now.

MRS. VOCKERAT.

Silly boy ! What I want, Jack, is that you should
be happy—a contented man, my son.

JOHN.

Ah, mother ! you'll never live to see that. The
contented people are nothing but the drones in the
hive. A worthless pack.

MRS. VOCKERAT.

But what's the good of all that if . . .

JOHN.

[More serious and with more animation.] That boy
in there, he's to be just such another, a thoroughly
discontented man.

MRS. VOCKERAT.

God forbid, Jack !

JOHN.

But he's to be a very different fellow from me. I'll take good care of that.

. MRS. VOCKERAT.

Man proposes and God disposes. We did our best.

JOHN.

Well, mammy, I'm not such a dreadful disappointment to you after all, am I ?

MRS. VOCKERAT.

Of course you're not. That's not what I mean—not at all. . . . But you say yourself that Philip is to be different. And—and—you know what I mean, John. You are an unbeliever . . . you don't even believe in God. You've really and truly no religion at all. That cannot fail to grieve us.

JOHN.

Religion, religion ! I certainly don't believe that God looks like a man, and acts like one, and that He has a son, and so on.

MRS. VOCKERAT.

But, John, we must believe that.

JOHN.

No, mother ! We can have a religion without believing such things. [*In a rather declamatory tone.*] Whoever seeks to know Nature seeks to know God. God *is* Nature.

" What were a God who ruled his world only from without ?
In space mechanically whirled the universe about ?
'Tis in the heart of things that He must live and move and
  rule."

That's what Goethe says, mammy, and he knew more about it than all the pastors and priests in the world put together.

MRS. VOCKERAT.

O boy, boy! When I hear you talk like that, I . . . It's a sad pity that ever you gave up the Church. I remember well what the Superintendent said to me after your trial sermon . . .

JOHN.

[*Amused.*] Mother, mother! that's a very old story now!

[*Door bell rings.*

MRS. VOCKERAT.

The door! I thought it was open. [*Takes a few steps towards door into entrance-hall.*]

[*Knock at this door. Enter timidly* MRS. LEHMANN, *the washerwoman, in a shabby, faded, blue print dress.*]

MRS. LEHMANN.

Good day t' you, ma'am. Good day t' you, sir.

MRS. VOCKERAT *and* JOHN.

[*Not quite simultaneously.*] Good day to you, Mrs. Lehmann.

MRS. LEHMANN.

You'll not take it amiss, if you please, 'm. I beg pardon, I'm sure. But it's my lodger gentleman I'm lookin' for, ma'am, this half-hour and more.

JOHN.

You've come to the right place at last, Mrs. Lehmann. Mr. Braun is here.

MRS. LEHMANN.

Thank you, sir. [*Looking round.*] Well, well! if this isn't beautiful!

MRS. VOCKERAT.

And how are you, Mrs. Lehmann?

MRS. LEHMANN.

O Mrs. Vockerat, ma'am, I've been but in a pore way lately. I've 'ad to send my old man off at last, m'm. It was beyond all bearin'! I'll 'ave to do for my five alone now, 'eaven 'elp me!

MRS. VOCKERAT.

You don't mean to tell me! But——

MRS. LEHMANN.

[*Talking faster and faster.*] You see, Mrs. Vockerat, ma'am, it would all be like nothing if I 'adn't sich pore 'ealth. But it's a pore sufferin' woman I am. And it's nothin' but 'is conduct that's done it, an' there's no one can't blame me. I says to my old man, says I, Thomas, says I, it's time now as you was a-takin' of yourself off. Go you and jine yourself to them as you belongs to, says I, them as you're for ever a-drinkin' with. Go you to them, says I. I'll keep my five children myself, if I've to work my fingers to the bone. See what you can get for *yourself*, says I, and then put it down your own throat as fast as ever it will go. What spirit is there in you? says I. If you had as much spirit as that! [*Snaps her fingers*] in your whole body, you wouldn't have brought your wife and children to sich a pass, says I. Yes, Mrs. Vockerat, m'm, them was my very words; it's as true as I'm standing here; and it went to my very heart to say them, it did—like a knife as you may say. But there was nothing else for it, and if you want me to tell the truth, ma'am, I'm 'eartily glad things is as they is! And I trusts as how the Lord will stand by me and my five pore children.

[*She sniffs and wipes her eyes.*

MRS. VOCKERAT.

If we only always . . .

MRS. LEHMANN.

My very words, ma'am; just what I said myself, ma'am! You go your ways, says I. Be off with you, says I. I'm an honest woman and one as can work, says I, and what's more, I can keep what I earns, says I, and there's no fear but what we'll get on somehow. And it's honest I am, Mrs. Vockerat, ma'am. No need to lock things away for me, ma'am —not as much as would go under my finger-nail . . .

JOHN.

Do you want to speak to Mr. Braun, Mrs. Lehmann?

MRS. LEHMANN.

Well I never! If I 'adn't clean forgot! There's a young lady here as would like to speak to 'im.

[MISS MAHR *puts her head in at the door leading from entrance-hall, but draws back again at once.* JOHN *has noticed it.*

JOHN.

Won't you come in? Please do. [*To his mother and* MRS. LEHMANN, *who have seen nothing.*] It was the young lady—she is there. [*To* MRS. LEHMANN.] You ought to have brought her in. [*He opens the door.*]

Please come in.   You want to speak to my friend
Braun, I know.

[*Enter* MISS ANNA MAHR. *She is twenty-*
four; middle height, with small head,
dark, smooth hair, and delicate, mobile
features. There is both grace and strength
in her unaffected movements. A certain
decision and liveliness of manner are
softened down by so much modesty and
tact that the impression of womanliness is
preserved. She is dressed in black.

MISS ANNA MAHR.

I must offer a thousand apologies.   I am exceedingly
sorry to intrude.

JOHN.

I assure you that you are not intruding in the very
least.

MISS MAHR.

Mrs. Lehmann seemed to be never coming back
again—and I only wanted to say to her—that . . . .
that I can easily look up Mr. Braun at another
time.

JOHN.

Not at all !   I'll call Braun this moment if you
will be good enough to take a seat.

MISS MAHR.

Thank you very much. [*Remains standing.*]   But
really I couldn't think of giving so much trouble ;
I . . .

JOHN.

It's not the slightest trouble !   I'll have Braun here
in a moment.

MISS MAHR.

No, I can't allow you to . . .

JOHN.

It's a pleasure. Excuse me one moment.

[Exit by verandah.

[Short embarrassed pause.]

MRS. LEHMANN.

Then I'll be off, miss. [*To* MISS MAHR.] You'll be able to find the way back alone.

MISS MAHR.

Thank you for coming with me. Here's something for the children. *[Gives her money.*

MRS. LEHMANN.

Thank you, miss, thank you ! [*To* MRS. VOCKERAT.] The first money that's touched my 'and this blessed day, ma'am ! And it's the truth I'm telling you ! No, ma'am, it's no easy matter, ma'am, but I'll rather, says I, sell myself for a negro slave, says I, than live any longer with such a drunken sot, such a . . . And we've the Lord to trust in, ma'am. And He's never deserted me yet. I'm off to the shop now, ma'am, to get something for my pore little children.

[Exit.

MRS. VOCKERAT.

[Calls after her.] Go into the kitchen, Mrs. Lehmann. They'll give you something there. *[Takes a chair herself beside the one* JOHN *has placed for* MISS MAHR.] Do sit down while you are waiting, won't you ?

MISS MAHR.

[Seats herself hesitatingly.] I am not at all tired, I . . .

MRS. VOCKERAT.

Do you know this neighbourhood well?

MISS MAHR.

No. I come from the Russian Baltic Provinces, I . . . *[Embarrassed pause.*

MRS. VOCKERAT.

The country about here is very sandy. I don't care for it myself. I'm from the neighourhood of Breslau. And you would hardly believe what a price everything is here! My husband has a large farm, so we can help the children by sending them things every now and then. . . . Have you seen the lake? Now that's really pretty—the lake *is* pretty, there's no denying it. And we're nice and near it, just on the shore. We have two boats down there at the other end of the garden. But I can't bear the children to go out rowing; I'm too nervous. May I ask if you are living in Berlin now?

MISS MAHR.

Yes. It's my first visit to Berlin. It is a place I have always wanted to see thoroughly.

MRS. VOCKERAT.

Oh yes! Berlin is well worth seeing. But it's very noisy.

MISS MAHR.

That it certainly is. Especially when one is accustomed to small towns.

MRS. VOCKERAT.

You come . . . if it is not a rude question?

MISS MAHR.

From Reval—but I'm on my way back to Zurich, where I have spent the last four years.

MRS. VOCKERAT.

Indeed! in Switzerland—beautiful Switzerland. You have relations in Zurich, I suppose?

MISS MAHR.

No, I am studying there.

MRS. VOCKERAT.

You don't say so! . . . Not at the university?

MISS MAHR.

Yes, at the university.

MRS. VOCKERAT.

Well, well, I never! You are a student, then? That's most interesting! A real student?

MISS MAHR.

Yes, certainly.

MRS. VOCKERAT.

Well, well! to think of that! And do you mean to tell me that you *like* all that learning?

MISS MAHR.

[*Amused.*] Oh yes, on the whole I do—to a certain extent.

MRS. VOCKERAT.

Is it possible?

[JOHN *and* BRAUN *appear on the verandah. The ladies see them and both rise.*

MISS MAHR.

Allow me to apologize once more, madam, for this intrusion.

C

MRS. VOCKERAT.

No need to do that. It has given me great pleasure to meet a real student for once. Plain people like us get stupid ideas into our heads sometimes. You are a relation of Mr. Braun's?

MISS MAHR.

No, we made each other's acquaintance in Paris, at the time of the Exhibition.

MRS. VOCKERAT.

[*Shakes hands with her.*] Good-bye ! It has really given me pleasure . . .

MISS MAHR.

And I do hope you'll excuse me.
[MRS. VOCKERAT *bows ; exit by door into entrance hall.*

[JOHN *and* BRAUN *have deliberated for a moment on the verandah, whereupon* JOHN *seats himself out on the verandah, and* BRAUN *enters.*

BRAUN.

[*Surprised.*] Miss Mahr! Can it be you?

MISS MAHR.

Yes, Mr. Braun—but I hope you won't think that I am so tactless as to . . It's the fault of that wonderful landlady of yours, Mrs. Lehmann, that I have followed you here.

BRAUN.

Great Cæsar !

MISS MAHR.

So *he's* alive yet ?

BRAUN.

It would never have occurred to me so much as to dream of this. It's perfectly ripping.

MISS MAHR.

Still ripping? Is everything ripping yet? I don't believe you have changed at all.

BRAUN.

Do you think not? But take off your things, Miss Mahr.

MISS MAHR.

Certainly not! What are you dreaming about, Mr. Braun? I only wanted to see how you were getting on. [*Teasingly.*] And specially to make inquiry about your great picture. Is it on view yet?

BRAUN.

It's not in existence yet, Miss Mahr, not even the canvas!

MISS MAHR.

That's bad, very bad. And you promised me so faithfully.

BRAUN.

Promises are like pie-crust, Miss Mahr. But do please, take off your things.

MISS MAHR.

Now I've seen you, I hope you'll . . .

BRAUN.

No, no, you must stay here.

MISS MAHR.

Here?

BRAUN.

Oh! by the bye, I forgot that you didn't know where
we are. This is John Vockerat's house. Old John
Vockerat—you have heard about him often enough
from me. And what's more, you have come in the
very nick of time. There's a christening on to-day.

MISS MAHR.

No, no! What nonsense you are talking! Besides,
I have several errands in town.

BRAUN.

The shops are all shut.

MISS MAHR.

That doesn't matter; it's only calls I have to make.
But don't suppose you have got rid of me, for all that.
We must meet again and have a talk. Besides, I
must give you a good scolding, you breaker of promises!
I see that you still paint your pictures only in imagi-
nation . . .

BRAUN.

It's no use beginning until one has come to a clear
understanding of what one wants to do. After that,
the mere painting is a comparative trifle

MISS MAHR.

That may be so!—possibly!

BRAUN.

You needn't think you're going away now, Miss
Mahr.

MISS MAHR.

Yes, indeed, Mr. Braun. I'll just slip quietly . . .

BRAUN.

[*Calls.*] Jack!! Jack!!!

Miss Mahr.

But, Mr. Braun!

[*Enter* John. *He blushes.*]

Braun.

Allow me! My friend John Vockerat—Miss Anna Mahr.

Miss Mahr *and* John.

[*Simultaneously.*] I have heard so much about you.

Braun.

Fancy, John!—Miss Mahr insists on going off again at once.

John.

My wife and all of us would be very sorry indeed if she did. Won't you stay and spend the afternoon with us?

Miss Mahr.

I don't know what to say. . . . If you are sure that it is really quite convenient, it will give me much pleasure to do so.

John.

Perfectly convenient, I assure you. [*He helps her to take off her cape, hands it to* Braun.] Hang that up, please! I must tell my wife. . . . [*Calls at the bed·room door.*] Kitty! [*Exit into bedroom.*

Miss Mahr.

[*Arranging her dress at the mirror.*] How kind your friend is!

Braun.

A little too kind, perhaps.

Miss Mahr.

Indeed—what do you mean ?

Braun.

I'm only joking. He's a real good fellow—except
that he can be a little tiresome when he gets on the
subject of his work. You bet he reads his book to
you if you stay here this afternoon.

Miss Mahr.

What's it about ?

Braun.

Much too learned for me. It's philosophical, critical,
psycho-physiological—I don't know what all!

Miss Mahr.

But this is very interesting. I'm a devotee of
philosophy myself.

Braun.

Then I can tell you you won't get away in a hurry.
He'll be tremendously pleased if you are interested in
his work.

John.

[*Enters from bedroom.*] Braun !

Braun.

Well ?

John.

Go and try if you can relieve Kitty's anxiety, will
you ? She thinks that one of the child's ribs is sticking out where it ought not to be.

Braun.

What !

JOHN.

It's nothing at all, but go to her.   She is worrying about it.

BRAUN.

All right!   I'll go. |*Exit into the bedroom.*

JOHN.

My wife begs you to excuse her, Miss Mahr.   She'll come in a few minutes.   She thinks you might like to see our little garden.   Do you care to take a walk round?

MISS MAHR.

I should like to, very much.

JOHN.

[*Smiling.*] We have quite a nice piece of ground— only rented though, you know.   The best thing about it is the pretty lake.   Do you know the Müggelsee? [*He hands her her parasol.   Both, talking, go towards verandah door.*] I'm one of the people who hate town life.   My ideal is a great park, well walled in. There one could devote one's self undisturbed to one's aims.

MISS MAHR.

Epicurean!

JOHN.

Yes, quite true!   But I assure you it is the only way in which I could possibly . . . Will you not be too cold?

MISS MAHR.

Oh no!   I am an open-air person.
[JOHN *lets* MISS MAHR *go first, and follows her on to the verandah, where both stand for a few momemts.*   JOHN *is seen show-*

ing and explaining the view. Then both disappear in the garden.

Enter BRAUN *from the bedroom, followed by* KITTY.

BRAUN.

[*Looks round.*] They've gone out.

KITTY.

Oh!

BRAUN.

No, no! that rib is in a perfectly natural position.

KITTY.

I have such a feeling of oppression.

BRAUN.

Oppression? Why?

KITTY.

[*Smiling.*] Regular palpitation of the heart.

BRAUN.

It's because you're not strong yet.

KITTY.

Is she very proud?

BRAUN.

Who?

KITTY.

Miss Mahr, I mean.

BRAUN.

Anna Mahr! Proud! Not a bit of it.

KITTY.

I know *I* should be, if I were . . .

BRAUN.

She's not! I can assure you. You do her injustice there.

KITTY.

Not at all! I have an unbounded respect for her.

BRAUN.

I don't know! . . . She can give herself airs on occasion. Then of course one has to take her down a bit. *[Pause.*

KITTY.

I see John has left a page of his manuscript lying there. Now, does she understand anything of that?

BRAUN.

I should rather think she did!

KITTY.

Really? Oh dear! It's a poor figure *we* make compared with these highly educated women.

BRAUN.

I'm not so sure of that!—I know little enough myself.—I'm not a university man. But I'm not overawed by any one's little bit of book-learning.

KITTY.

She's a brilliant talker, I've no doubt.

BRAUN.

Brilliant? No. She talks . . . very like the rest of us. She's undoubtedly clever; but that—isn't everything.

KITTY.

[Smiling.] As a girl I was a perfect chatterbox. My tongue went from morning to night about

nothing at all. I've cured myself of that, anyhow. But now I make the opposite mistake; now I hardly dare to speak at all. [*Calls out at the verandah door.*] Mammy! you must make room for one more!

MRS. VOCKERAT.

[*From the verandah, where she is rearranging the table.*] Who's coming?

KITTY.

The young lady—Mr. Braun's friend.

MRS. VOCKERAT.

Who? Yes, yes, I remember. I'll see to it, Kitty.

KITTY.

[*Turns towards* BRAUN *again; sighs.*] Yes! It's past all mending! One does one's best—but it's no good—it's too late! [*Stands examining a vase of roses.*] Look how beautiful these are. Fancy having roses still! [*Holds them for* BRAUN *to smell.*] And with such a delicious scent too!

BRAUN.

Delicious!

KITTY.

[*Returns the vase to its place.*] Is she young?

BRAUN.

Who?

KITTY.

Miss Mahr.

BRAUN.

I really don't know her age.

KITTY.

I'm twenty-two already—going down the hill!

BRAUN.

Fast. [*Laughs.*]

KITTY.

I know well what an ignorant, narrow-minded creature I am!

> [MRS. VOCKERAT *puts her head in at the door.*]

MRS. VOCKERAT.

Everything is ready. [*Withdaws. Calls from the verandah into the garden.*] Papa! Papa!

MR. VOCKERAT *and* PASTOR KOLLIN, *both in excellent spirits, come up the verandah steps.*

VOCKERAT.

[*At the open door, with the* PASTOR'S *overcoat on his arm.*] Come along, sir! Come in and let me hang up your things. Ha, ha, ha! [*Laughs heartily.*]

PASTOR KOLLIN.

[*Carrying his hat, muffler, and stick, smoking and laughing, interjects.*] Ha, ha, ha! too funny, you know! Pf, pf—never heard anything so funny. [*Laughs.*]

VOCKERAT.

And it's said to be a perfectly true story, Mr. Kollin. [*Hangs up overcoat.*

PASTOR KOLLIN.

" Mr. Becker! " [*Laughs.*]—pf, pf—" Mr. Becker! anything else wanted, sir ? " [*Laughs; hangs up hat and muffler; keeps on skull-cap.*]

VOCKERAT.

[*Laughing too.*] Mr. Becker. . . . [*To* BRAUN.] It was at a funeral in the country, in our neighbourhood, Mr. Braun. The mourners were all standing round the coffin. [*Quickly, with pantomime of fright.*] All at once something is heard to move. Very likely it was only a chair creaking, or—anyhow something moves. [*Pantomime of horror.*] Every one starts. The beadle is the only man to keep his head—ha, ha, ha!—he's the brave one. He goes cautiously up to the coffin—ha, ha, ha!—and knocks. [*Imitating the beadle's voice, and knocking on the table with his knuckles.*]—"Mr. Becker!—Mr. Becker! anything else wanted, sir?" [*Fit of hearty laughing.*]

PASTOR KOLLIN.

[*Laughing.*] Yes, yes!—pf, pf!—that's genuine! I know these beadles.

MRS. VOCKERAT.

[*Comes in from verandah.*] Now, papa, come along! Don't let the soup get cold.

VOCKERAT.

Mr. Kollin, will you be so good . . .

PASTOR KOLLIN.

I really ought not to be here, you know! [*He puts the end of his cigar into the ash-tray, then offers* MRS. VOCKERAT *his arm.*] May I have the pleasure, Mrs. Vockerat?

VOCKERAT.

[*In the act of giving his arm to his daughter-in-law.*] But where is John?

MRS. VOCKERAT.

And our young lady? This is too bad of John.
Dinner will be . . .

VOCKERAT.

[*Jovially.*] How true it is, Mr. Kollin : " There's
many a slip "—ha, ha, ha !

PASTOR KOLLIN.

" Between the cup and the lip "—ha, ha, ha !

VOCKERAT.

Yes, that must have been the lady. We saw a
young couple out on the lake. Didn't we, Mr. Kollin ?

PASTOR KOLLIN.

We did, sir, we did ! They must have gone for a
row.

MRS. VOCKERAT.

Then I think we'll begin without them !

VOCKERAT.

Nothing like punctuality.

BRAUN.

[*Who has been looking out from the verandah, comes
in.*] Here they are ! Here they come !

VOCKERAT.

And just about time they did !

Enter JOHN *and* MISS MAHR *from the verandah.*

JOHN.

Are we very late?

VOCKERAT.

No, you're in time yet.

JOHN.

I'm very sorry; we had . . . it was so splendid on the lake. . . . Allow me! [*Introducing.*] The Reverend Mr. Kollin. My father. My mother.

MRS. VOCKERAT.

I have already had the pleasure.

JOHN.

My wife—Miss Mahr.

> [*Exeunt all on to the verandah,* MRS. VOCKERAT *taking* PASTOR KOLLIN'S *arm,* KITTY *her father-in-law's,* JOHN *giving his to* MISS MAHR. BRAUN, *alone, brings up the rear. The stage is empty. The* NURSE, *in the bedroom, is heard singing softly: Hush-a-bye, baby. Sound of plates, knives, and forks comes from the verandah. Enter* KITTY *hurriedly, to fetch something from a table-drawer, quickly followed by* JOHN.

JOHN.

Now, Kitty—you know you're not to—you know you oughtn't to run. Do let me . . .

KITTY.

I'm not so weak as all that.

JOHN.

[*Wildly enthusiastic.*] I say, Kitty, that's a splendid girl! Stores of learning! Wonderful originality! And to think that such a woman has barely enough to exist upon! At least, so Braun has always told us. I declare I think it's our bounden duty to ask her to stay with us for a few weeks.

KITTY.

As you like, John.

JOHN.

It's not I. It's you that ought to want it. It's of far greater importance to you than to me. You can learn no end from a woman like that.

KITTY.

I must say you're rather horrid sometimes, John.

JOHN.

But is it not true? You ought to be tremendously keen to seize every chance of educating your mind a little. To leave no stone unturned! Certainly you ought to try to get her to stay. I can't understand how any one can be so indifferent.

KITTY.

But I'm quite pleased that she should stay, John.

JOHN.

No one has a spark of spirit! no one has any initiative!—It's awful!

[PASTOR KOLLIN, *outside, knocks on his glass.*

KITTY.

Do go, John! Mr. Kollin is proposing a toast. I'm coming this moment. You may be sure I'm quite pleased about it. But we can't both be away when . . .

JOHN.

Come now, Kitty, don't, don't! [*He kisses away the tears from her eyes and hurries on to the verandah.*]
[*The* PASTOR's *voice is heard. Also the gentle sound of the* NURSE's *lullaby. A change comes over* KITTY. *As soon as* JOHN *has*

gone, she seems to turn faint, and has to catch hold of things to support herself by as she tries to make her way back to the verandah. She becomes giddy, can go no farther, and has to sit down. Stares vacantly; moves her lips without making any sound. Eyes full of tears. The PASTOR's *speech comes to an end. Glasses are touched.* KITTY *recovers herself, rises, moves on towards the verandah.*

END OF THE FIRST ACT

THE SECOND ACT

[*Beautiful autumn morning.* MRS. VOCKERAT, *in print dress, with apron and bunch of keys, is arranging the breakfast-table. A party of men passing the house are singing:* "*Waving wood, who built thee high?*" MISS ANNA MAHR, *with a basket of grapes on her arm, appears on the verandah from the garden. She stands for a moment listening to the singing, and then, shading her eyes with her hand, looks across the lake into the distance. She wears a black wrapper with short sleeves. Black lace scarf thrown over head and neck. Bunch of bright autumn leaves fastened in her dress. She turns and comes in.*

MRS. VOCKERAT.

Good morning, Miss Anna.

MISS MAHR.

[*Lays down her basket, hurries towards* MRS. VOCKERAT, *and kisses her hand.*] Good morning, Mama Vockerat.

MRS. VOCKERAT.

Up so early, Miss Anna?

MISS MAHR.

We are gathering the grapes, Dr. Vockerat and I.

D

MRS. VOCKERAT.

It's certainly time they were in. [*Takes one or two from the basket and tastes them.*] They won't turn any sweeter now.—But are you not cold, Miss Anna? [*Touches* MISS MAHR'S *bare arm with her finger.*] You're rather lightly dressed? . . . And the air seems sharp this morning.

MISS MAHR.

[*Occupied in spreading out the bunches of grapes carefully on a board.*] It's nice and keen. I don't mind that. ✦ Cold suits me. ✻ The air is delicious.— The stakes in the lake—I mean the stakes the boats are fastened to—they were white with hoar-frost— early this morning:—it looked quite beautiful. But everything here is beautiful. . . . Can I do anything to help you now, Mama Vockerat?

MRS. VOCKERAT.

If you wouldn't mind handing me over the sugar- basin.

MISS MAHR.

[*Has placed the sugar-basin on the table. Still bending over it, looks up sideways.*] You are not angry when I call you Mama Vockerat, are you?

MRS. VOCKERLT.

[*Laughs.*] Why should that make me angry?

MISS MAHR.

It makes me so happy that you allow me to do it. [*Impetuously kisses* MRS. VOCKERAT.] I can't tell you how grateful I am to you for allowing me to be here.

MRS. VOCKERAT.

Oh, Miss Anna!

MISS MAHR.

I feel so happy with you all. You are all so sweet to me. You are such good people.

MRS. VOCKERAT.

Now did any one . . . ! You are covered with spiders' webs. [*Picks the threads off* ANNA'S *dress.*]

MISS MAHR.

It's such a happy life, this family life. I·never knew what it was before.

MRS. VOCKERAT.

[*Still picking off threads.*] Don't say too much, Miss Anna, it's not lucky. Stop a minute!—look at this . . . regular strings!

MISS MAHR.

Are you superstitious, Mama Vockerat?

MRS. VOCKERAT.

Not I, my dear! We know that we may trust in God's goodness. Yet things are not everything one could wish them to be.

MISS MAHR.

You don't really mean that.—I'm sure you are all . . . . No, no! you must not say that!

MRS. VOCKERAT.

You are quite right. I won't say it. It is wrong of me to grumble. [*Changes the subject.*] We are all enjoying having you with us. [*Mysteriously.*] You do John so much good.

Miss Mahr.

[*Surprised ; changes colour ; suddenly and eagerly.*]
Do you really like me a little, then ?

Mrs. Vockerat.

I like you very much, dear.

Miss Mahr.

But not so much as I do you. I love you as if you
were my own mother. [*Takes up the basket, in the
act of returning to the garden.*] Dr. Vockerat is so
kind ; he is almost too tender-hearted.

Mrs. Vockerat.

In what way ?

Miss Mahr.

Why, in every way! Yesterday, for instance, we
met a tipsy man in the street. The children were
just coming out of school, and the grown-up people
too were teasing him. Quite a crowd had collected in
front of the town-hall . . .

Mrs. Vockerat.

I know! That's the very sort of thing John can't
bear. It maddens him. He has often got himself
into trouble by interfering.

Miss Mahr.

And do you not admire him for it, Mama Vockerat ?

Mrs. Vockerat.

Admire him ? Well—perhaps I do. He's certainly
a kind-hearted fellow. But when you come to think,
what's the good of it ? Kind-hearted he may be, but
what of that ? He has forgotten his God. That's
no small grief, I can assure you, Miss Mahr, to a

mother . . . to parents—who have, I may say, made
it the object of their lives to bring up their son to be
a true Christian. [*She blows her nose to hide her
emotion.*] I have had a wretched cold for several
days. . . . [*Occupied in dusting; after a pause.*] He
is a good boy, and of course we are thankful for that,
and yet it only makes it all doubly sad. And it's
easy to see that he's being punished already—there is
no blessing on his labours. Always at it! restless
and hurried! And all to no purpose, for it's plain
enough that he doesn't get on.—And what a child he
was! . . . A perfect wonder! I remember Pastor
Schmidt . . . He surprised every one. In the Fifth
Form when he was thirteen—done with school at six-
teen—and now? Now most of them have left him
far behind. Some that were not half so clever got
good appointments long ago.

Miss Mahr.

The thing seems so natural to me. It simply proves
that Dr. Vockerat is not content to follow the beaten
track. Some people must work unfettered. Dr.
Vockerat is one of those who are striking out new
paths.

Mrs. Vockerat.

But there's nothing to be gained by that, Miss
Anna! He's only wearing himself out. I'd a hundred
times rather see him a plain farmer—or a gardener—
or in any other small way, if he could only give up
that brood-brooding. . . . But don't let me make you
sad, Miss Anna. I can't help feeling overwhelmed
sometimes, as if it were almost more than I could bear.
Then when I've grieved over things for a bit, I say to
myself again: God will order everything for the

best. Yes, yes! you smile at that. I'm an old-
fashioned woman. I put my trust in Him—in Him
that's above, I mean : no power on earth can separate
me from Him.

Miss Mahr.

I'd never wish it to. And I was not smiling,
Mama Vockerat. And now you are quite cheerful
again yourself. Come out for a little, won't you?
It's lovely out on the verandah.

Mrs. Vockerat.

No, no! I should catch cold. Besides, I have
other things to do. You go—and bring in John.
Breakfast is ready.   [*Exit* Miss Mahr.

> [Mrs. Vockerat *goes on dusting. The sound
> of fifes and drums is heard. She hurries
> to the window. The sounds die away
> gradually.*

Enter Kitty, *in a morning wrapper, from bedroom.*

Kitty.

[*Languidly.*] There are far too many people about
on Sundays.

Mrs. Vockerat.

That was a gymnastic club from Berlin, Kitty.
Splendid strong fellows! Good morning, child.
How have you slept? You don't look particularly
well.

Kitty.

Baby woke me twice, and it was a long time before
I fell asleep again. Stop, mother! I must try to
remember . . . I must think.

Mrs. Vockerat.

I'm sure you ought to give in, child, and let nurse take baby at night.

Kitty.

[*Gently reproachful.*] Oh mother! you know! . . .

Mrs. Vockerat.

But why not?

Kitty.

You know I won't do that.

Mrs. Vockerat.

You'll likely be obliged to do it in the end.

Kitty.

[*Annoyed.*] I will not be separated from him— from my own child. A poor little baby without a mother . . .

Mrs. Vockerat.

Now Kitty, Kitty! who ever thought of such a thing? Come, come! I must get you something— shall it be coffee? And shall I butter a roll for you, or . . .

Kitty.

[*Sitting at the table, exhausted.*] Thank you, mother, if it's not too much trouble. [Mrs. Vockerat *butters the roll; after a pause,* Kitty *continues.*] But where is John?

Mrs. Vockerat.

They are taking in the grapes; he and Miss Anna.

Kitty.

[*Resting her chin on her hand; eagerly.*] She is nice, mother, isn't she?

MRS. VOCKERAT.

Yes, I must say I like her.

KITTY.

And yet, mother, you know you would never allow a word to be said in favour of the New Woman.

MRS. VOCKERAT.

Still one must be fair, and there's no denying that . . .

KITTY.

[*Musingly.*] So gentle and womanly. Never puts herself forward, though she knows so much, and is so clever all round. That's what I admire in her. Don't you, mammy? That she never makes any show of her learning. . . . I've been quite happy about John lately. Don't you notice, mother, that he's always so cheerful now?

MRS. VOCKERAT.

[*Surprised.*] Yes, dear, you're right. He's sometimes in quite high spirits.

KITTY.

Isn't he, mammy?

MRS. VOCKERAT.

That's because he has got some one to hold forth to on these learned subjects of his.

KITTY.

Which is of the greatest importance to him.

MRS. VOCKERAT.

No doubt! no doubt! [*Pause.*

KITTY.

I agree with Miss Mahr on many points. She was

saying lately that we women live in a condition of
degradation. I think she's quite right there. It is
what I feel very often.

Mrs. Vockerat.

Oh, these are matters I don't trouble about. And
she knows better, too, than to talk that way to an old
experienced woman like me. I'm too old and I've
seen too much.

Kitty.

But she's right, mother. It's as clear as daylight
that she's right. We are really and truly a despised
and ill-used sex. Only think that there is still a law
—so she told me yesterday—which allows the husband
to inflict a certain amount of corporal punishment on
his wife.

Mrs. Vockerat.

I didn't know that. And I'll not discuss the matter.
I daresay it's nothing so very bad. But if you want
to please me, Kitty, don't meddle with these new
ideas. They do nothing but confuse people, and
destroy their peace of mind.—I'm going for your
coffee, child.—That's my opinion, Kitty. [*Exit.*

> [Kitty *sits with her elbow on the table, resting
> her chin on her hand.* John *and* Miss
> Mahr, *talking loudly and laughing,
> suddenly pass the windows.* Kitty *starts,
> trembles, and rises to look after them, with
> an anxious expression and breathing hard.*
> Mrs. Vockerat *is heard coming with the
> coffee. She enters and finds* Kitty *at the
> table in the position in which she left
> her.*

MRS. VOCKERAT.

[*Pours out coffee.*] There now, that will revive you.

Enter MISS MAHR *and* JOHN *from the verandah.*

MRS. VOCKERAT.

That's right. You're just in time.

JOHN.

[*Leaves the door open.*] We'll not shut the door. The sun is quite warm already.—Have you hurt yourself badly, Miss Anna?

MISS MAHR.

[*Drawing some long vine sprays after her.*] No, not at all. The espalier was so wet that I slipped, but I let the scissors go. [*Hastens to* KITTY, *takes both her hands and kisses her on her forehead.*] Good morning, Mrs. John. Oh, what cold hands you have!— --
[*Rubs her hands to warm them.*

JOHN.

[*Kisses* KITTY'S *cheek from behind.*] Good morning, Kitty! [*Affecting surprise, jocularly.*] Heavens! what does she look like again! Miserable! Like some poor little sick chicken!

MRS. VOCKERAT.

It's you that are bringing the cold in with you. It is almost time we had fires. But come along now!
[*Has poured out coffee for all.*

MISS MAHR.

[*Decorates the table with her vine sprays.*] Something pretty.

KITTY.

How lovely!

JOHN.

[*Takes his seat.*] I put it to you both: is Miss Anna not a different creature to-day from what she was a week ago—when she arrived?

MISS MAHR.

I am too well off here. I really ought not to stay longer.

MRS. VOCKERAT.

The country air agrees with her.

JOHN.

And who was it that would not, and would not . . .

MRS. VOCKERAT.

I wonder what papa is doing?

JOHN.

Counting the time till you come back to him.

MRS. VOCKERAT.

Not so bad as that. He has plenty to do. The winter wheat is sown now, that's true; still, he wrote that I was to stay as long as I was needed.

JOHN.

He'll come for you, mother, won't he?

MRS. VOCKERAT.

Yes, whenever I write. [*To* MISS MAHR.] He is glad of any opportunity to see the children again. And now there's the little grandson, too! I'll never forget his excitement the morning your telegram came: " Fine boy." The old man was almost out of his mind with joy.

KITTY.

Dear papa! You must really go back to him soon.
It would be too selfish of us . . .

MRS. VOCKERAT.

That's all very fine! You get some colour into
your cheeks first.

MISS MAHR.

I should be here! You mustn't undervalue me!
I know all about housekeeping. You have no idea
what fine dishes I could cook for you—Russian ones!
—Borschtsch or pillau.

[*All laugh.*

MRS. VOCKERAT.

[*With unconscious eagerness.*] No, no! I'm certainly
not going yet.

KITTY.

Well, mother, if it's really not asking too much of
you . . .

[*Pause.*

JOHN.

Give me the honey, Kitty.

KITTY.

Why, here comes Braun!

Enter BRAUN *; overcoat, hat, umbrella, travelling-
bag, book under his arm. Bored expression.
Drags himself along weariedly.*

BRAUN.

Morning!

JOHN.

Where the deuce are *you* off to so early?

[MRS. VOCKERAT *flaps her table-napkin at something.*

JOHN.

It's a bee, mother! Don't kill it! don't kill it!

BRAUN.

I was going to Berlin—to fetch colours from my diggings. Missed the train, worse luck!

JOHN.

Not the first time, Breo!

BRAUN.

There's always to-morrow to fall back on.

KITTY.

[*Throws up her hands as if the bee were buzzing round her plate.*] It smells the honey.

MISS MAHR.

Are there no other trains? [*Looks down at the bouquet she is wearing: threateningly.*] Little bee, little bee!

BRAUN.

They are too dear for me. I never travel in any but workmen's trains.

JOHN.

And they only go quite early. But you can get on with your painting, can't you?

BRAUN.

Without paints? No.

JOHN.

Breo, Breo! you're falling into lazy habits, my boy.

BRAUN.

Famous one day sooner or one day later . . . But really ! painting altogether . . .

JOHN.

Chess-playing is more to your mind, eh ?

BRAUN.

Good for you if you had any such tastes. But your sea, my son, has no harbours. There's no rest in your life.

JOHN.

Oh, one cannot !——

MRS. VOCKERAT.

[*Jumps up, screams.*] A wasp, a wasp !

[*All get up and flap their table-napkins at the wasp.*

JOHN.

There ! it's gone.

MRS. VOCKERAT.

[*Sits down again.*] Horrid creatures !

[*All return to their places.*

JOHN.

[*To* BRAUN.] Sit down, won't you ?—What have you got there ?

BRAUN.

Oh, you would like to know, would·you ? Something interesting.

JOHN.

Have some more breakfast.

BRAUN.

[*Seats himself and gives the book to* JOHN, *who turns*

over the leaves.] Thanks, I'll be very glad of some. I had only time . . . Look at "The Artists"—by Garschin . . .

JOHN.

[*Turning over the leaves.*] What have you fished out now?

BRAUN.

The very thing for you, Jack.

MISS MAHR.

Yes, it is an excellent story. Had you not read it before?

BRAUN.

No, I only began it in bed this morning. That was what made me miss the train.

MISS MAHR.

Well, do you side with Rjäbinin or with Djedoff?

JOHN.

Anyhow, you are on the side of reading just now as against painting.

BRAUN.

Say rather that I am for the moment on neither. Read Garschin's story yourself, and take it to heart a little. There is work to be done at present that is probably of more importance than all the painting and writing in the world.

MISS MAHR.

I see, then, that you side with Rjäbinin.

BRAUN.

With Rjäbinin? Oh! I can't say at all decidedly that I do.

JOHN.

What is this story, " The Artists " ?

MISS MAHR.   ‹ · ·

It describes two artists — one a simple-minded
man, the other given to brooding. The simple-
minded man began life as an engineer, and turned
painter. The thinker gives up painting and turns
schoolmaster.

JOHN.

Why ?

MISS MAHR.

Because at the moment it seems to him to be of so
much more importance that there should be school-
masters than painters.

JOHN.

What leads him to the decision ?

MISS MAHR.

[*Has taken the book, turns the pages.*] Wait a
moment. The simplest way is for me to read you the
passage. Here it is. [*Turns, marking the place with
her finger, and explains to all.*] Djedoff, the former
engineer, is taking Rjäbinin over a boiler factory.
The men who have to work in the inside of the
boilers almost all turn deaf in course of time, from
the terrible noise of hammering. In Russia they
are known among the other workmen by the name
of " the deaf men." Djedoff points out to Rjäbinin
such a " deaf man " at work. [*Reads.*] " There he
was before my eyes, cowering in the dark depths of
the boiler, clothed in rags, almost overpowered with
fatigue. . . . his face dark crimson . . . the sweat
pouring from him . . . his broad, sunken breast
heaving painfully."

MRS. VOCKERAT.

What ever is the good of describing such dreadful things ? It can give pleasure to no one.

JOHN.

[*Laughs, strokes his mother's head caressingly.*] We can't be always laughing, can we, mammy ?

MRS. VOCKERAT.

I don't say that. But we may surely expect to get pleasure from art.

JOHN.

We can get much more from art than pleasure.

MISS MAHR.

It was not pleasure that Rjäbinin felt. He was painfully distressed, his innermost soul was stirred.

JOHN.

Think of the ground, mother—how it has to be torn up with the plough—every year—if it is to grow anything new.

MISS MAHR.

Something new sprang up in Rjäbinin. He said to himself: As long as such misery exists, it is a crime to work at anything which has not for its direct object the alleviation, the prevention of this misery.

MRS. VOCKERAT.

Yet it always has existed.

JOHN.

There was not much point in his turning schoolmaster.

E

BRAUN.

Do you think not ?   Is that not more useful work
than painting pictures and writing books ?

JOHN.

I don't know what your opinion of your profession
may be, but speaking for myself, I think very highly
of mine.

BRAUN.

You don't acknowledge it to yourself, and I do ;
that's all.

JOHN.

What's all ?   What do I not acknowledge to
myself ?

BRAUN.

· Why, that !

JOHN.

What ?

BRAUN.

That all that scribbling of yours is every bit as
useless as . . .

JOHN.

What scribbling ?

BRAUN.

Well, that psycho-physiological stuff.

JOHN.

[*Roughly.*] You know nothing whatever about it.

BRAUN.

And care less.

JOHN.

There you simply proclaim yourself to be a pitiful
ignoramus, a man of no education, a . . .

BRAUN.

That's right. Brag of your learning again.

JOHN.

You know very well that I don't give a farthing for my learning. But it is self-evident that . . .

BRAUN.

You are for ever saying that, and all the time the arrogance of superior education is streaming out at every pore. We'll let the subject alone! These are ticklish matters, which every man must settle for himself.

JOHN.

What do you mean by ticklish ?

BRAUN.

It's no good beginning, Jack. You can't stand an argument. You'll lose your temper again and . . .

JOHN.

I beg you'll explain yourself ! Say plainly what you mean.

BRAUN.

Oh, stuff! There's nothing to be gained by that. Let every one manage his own affairs.

JOHN.

And you think I manage mine badly, eh ?

BRAUN.

No worse than other people. You temporize, that's all.

JOHN.

You must excuse my not replying—it's a subject I'm sick of——[*Breaks out excitedly.*] This is how

the matter stands : You good friends of mine,˙ you
have threshed out a set of Radical catchwords for
yourselves, and because I have said to you once for
all that I refuse to use them, therefore I'm a
temporizer.

BRAUN.

That's your way of putting it—now listen to mine :
When the rest of us carried our opinions, regardless
of consequences, to their logical conclusion, you
turned against us and defended the old, the obsolete,
in every shape.   And it was by doing this that you
drove away your friends and isolated yourself.

KITTY.

[*Soothingly.*] John !

JOHN.

The friends that I could drive away—such friends,
to tell the truth—such friends I snap my fingers at.

BRAUN.

[*Rises.*] You snap your fingers at them ? [*Looks at*
ANNA.] When did you begin to do that, Jack ?

KITTY.

[*After a pause.*] Are you off already, Mr. Braun ?

BRAUN,

[*Offended, in an indifferent voice.*] Yes, I have
something to do.

JOHN.

[*Good-humouredly.*] Don't be silly !

BRAUN.

It's quite true.

JOHN.

In that case—I suppose you must go.

BRAUN.

Good morning !   [*Exit.*
                              [*Pause.*]

MRS. VOCKERAT.

[*Begins to collect the breakfast things.*] I don't know !
You're all so infatuated about that Braun.   I must
confess that I think very little of him.

JOHN.

[*Irritably.*]   Mother!   Will   you   do   me   the
favour . . .

KITTY.

But really, Braun is not at all nice to you, John.

JOHN.

Good people, I must beg of you not to interfere in
my private affairs.

             [*Pause. MRS. VOCKERAT clears away the
                breakfast things. KITTY rises.*

JOHN.

[*To* KITTY.]   Where are you going ?

KITTY.

To give baby his bath. [*Nods and smiles constrainedly
to* ANNA ; *exit into bedroom.*]

             [MRS. VOCKERAT, *carrying some of the break-
                fast things on a tray, is going towards the
                door into entrance-hall, when it is half-
                opened by a market-woman, who calls in :
                "Any vegetables to-day ? "*

MRS. VOCKERAT.

[*Answers.*]   I'm coming.

             [*Exit by door into entrance-hall.*
             [*Pause.*]

MISS MAHR.

[*Rises, sets her watch.*] I wonder what o'clock it is
—exactly? [*Turns to* JOHN, *who is still seated, looking
annoyed.*] Well, Dr. Vockerat!

> [*She hums the tune of "Cheer, boys, cheer,"
> looking archly at* JOHN. *Both burst out
> laughing.*

JOHN.

[*Serious again, sighs.*]   Ah, Miss Anna! it's sad,
sober earnest, I'm sorry to say.

MISS MAHR.

[*Shakes her finger threateningly at him.*] Be sure
you don't laugh, then!

JOHN.

[*Laughs again, then seriously.*] No, but really, you
don't know all that it means, all that lies behind a
speech like that of Braun's.

MISS MAHR.

Have you ever heard me play?

JOHN.

No, Miss Mahr!—I understood that you did not
play.

MISS MAHR.

Of course I don't!   I'm only joking.—By the bye,
are we not going for a row this morning?

JOHN.

I don't seem to care about anything now.

MISS MAHR.

[*Threateningly.*]   Dr. Vockerat!   Dr. Vockerat!
Why be depressed by such a trifle?

JOHN.

I can't understand how a man like Braun . . .

MISS MAHR.

Did what he said really make such a deep impression on you ?

JOHN.

It recalled all sorts of old unpleasantnesses, and . . .

MISS MAHR.

Forget them, Dr. Vockerat—the old unpleasantnesses. There is no real progress made so long as one is always looking back.

JOHN.

I believe you are right. And so we'll let that alone.—But is it not a curious thing, the way in which quite clever people can stick for years to a wrong opinion ? He means what he says. He looks on my scientific work as simple waste of time. Can you imagine such a thing ?

MISS MAHR.

There are such people.

JOHN.

Nothing will satisfy them but public activity, agitation, loud proclamation of one's opinions. Such a thing as a religious marriage ceremony is not to be thought of, not even as a concession to the orthodox upbringing of one's bride. They throw to the winds all respect for things or persons ; and a man like me, who shuts himself up in his study and lives a life of devotion to science, is in the eyes of his friends a man who has deserted his flag. Is that not extraordinary, Miss Mahr ?

Miss Mahr.

Dr. Vockerat, don't let it be of such importance to you what your friends think. If your opinions satisfy yourself, let it be a matter of indifference to you whether they satisfy others or not. These constant conflicts sap a man's strength.

John.

I know, I know! And I promise you that in future I'll not allow myself to be disturbed by their opinion of me. They must take me as I am, or let me alone! But you can't wonder at my having minded sometimes. One grows up with one's friends, and gets into the habit of expecting a little approbation from them. The feeling that that is completely withdrawn is like the feeling of trying to breathe in a vacuum.

Miss Mahr.

But you have your own family, Dr. Vockerat.

John.

Of course I have. Certainly. That is . . . Miss Anna! I know you will not misunderstand me. I have never spoken about it to any one before. You know how attached I am to them all. But, in what concerns my work, my own people are of no assistance to me whatever. Kitty undoubtedly has all the good-will in the world—in fact, it's most touching, the way she tries. And she praises everything. But I know that her verdict is worthless—so what help is it to me? And that's why I have lived in a sort of seventh heaven since you have been here, Miss Anna. It is the first time in my life that any one has taken an understanding, what may be called a professional, interest in my work, in any possible achievement of mine. It gives me fresh life. It's like rain on the dry ground. It is . . .

MISS MAHR.

You're getting absolutely poetical, Dr. Vockerat!

JOHN.

It's quite enough to make one poetical. But you are wrong about my family, Miss Anna. My mother positively hates the sight of my poor manuscript. Nothing would give her greater pleasure than to put it in the fire. It is equally objectionable to my father. You would hardly call that encouragement. As a matter of fact, my family hinder rather than help me. And after all that's not to be wondered at. But that one's friends should not show the very slightest appreciation of one's work—that a man like Braun . . .

MISS MAHR.

I cannot understand why Braun's disapproval, of all others, should affect you so much.

JOHN.

Well, with Braun, you see, it's this way. . . . We have known each other since we were boys.

MISS MAHR.

You mean that you have known *him*.

JOHN.

Yes, and he me.

MISS MAHR.

Are you quite sure of that?

JOHN.

Yes—that is, up to a certain point.

MISS MAHR.

It seems to me that your characters are so essentially different.

JOHN.

Do you really think so ?

MISS MAHR.

[*After a pause.*] Mr. Braun is still so undeveloped in every way—so . . . I don't exactly mean that he is jealous of you, but he is provoked . . . your fixed determination to go your own way annoys him. It even frightens him a little.—He has got the name of holding certain ethical or social opinions—call them what you like; to these he sticks, to these he clings, because he cannot stand alone. Like many men of the artistic temperament, he has no strong individuality. He needs to be supported. He must know that he has numbers at his back.

JOHN.

Oh, that some one had given me such advice long ago, in the days when the censure of my friends was almost more than I could bear ! Oh, that some one had spoken so to me then, when I was in utter despair ; when I reproached myself for living in a comfortable house, for having good food and clothing ; when it gave me a guilty feeling to meet a labouring man, and my heart beat as I slunk past the houses where the masons were at work ! I led my poor Kitty a pretty life in those days ! I wanted to give away everything and live with her a life of voluntary poverty. Rather than go through such a time again, I would—I would throw myself into the Müggelsee.

[*He seizes his hat.*] Now I must go and make that stupid fellow Braun listen to reason.

[Miss Mahr *looks as him with a peculiar smile.*

JOHN.

Do you not approve?

Miss Mahr.

If you must, then go by all means, you big child!

JOHN.

Miss Anna!

Miss Mahr.

Your own heart, Dr. Vockerat, is your greatest ✔ enemy.

JOHN.

But I have no peace as long as I think that he is going about feeling vexed and angry.

Miss Mahr.

Do you think it is a good thing to be so dependent?

JOHN.

[*Decidedly.*] No—it is not. I know he'll not come back again. He never was the first to make up. But that doesn't matter! You are right; and I'm not going after Braun—this time. We'll have that row on the lake now, Miss Mahr, if you feel inclined.

Miss Mahr.

But you were going to read me the third chapter.

JOHN.

We might take the manuscript with us.

MISS MAHR.

That would be very nice. I'll go and get ready at once. [*Exit.*
[JOHN *goes to the bookcase, takes out his manuscript, and is at once absorbed in it.*

Enter MRS. VOCKERAT *from hall, carrying two small gilt-edged books.*

MRS. VOCKERAT.

Here I come to take possession of one of the most comfortable chairs, put on my spectacles, and hold my little morning service. Is it warm enough to sit out on the verandah?

JOHN.

Certainly, mother. [*Looks up from the manuscript.*] What have you there?

MRS. VOCKERAT.

"Heart Echoes." You know—my favourite Lavater. And this other is Gerok's "Palm Leaves." What a man that Gerok was! He didn't spare the scientific people.—Oh dear! [*Puts her arm round* JOHN, *and rests her head on his shoulders. Tenderly.*] Well, my own boy! brooding again already? [*Half jestingly.*] Young father!

JOHN.

[*Looks up absently from the manuscript.*] Yes, mother?

MRS. VOCKERAT.

Do you not feel different now that you are a father, Jack?

JOHN.

No, mammy; much the same as usual.

MRS. VOCKERAT.

Come, come! don't pretend. First you could do nothing but jump for joy, and now . . . You don't mean to tell me you are discontented again?

JOHN.

[*Looks up absently.*] Perfectly contented, mammy.

MRS. VOCKERAT.

You are wearing that good suit every day, John, and you ought to wear out your old clothes here. I'm sure Miss Anna wouldn't mind.

JOHN.

Mother, I'm not a child now!

MRS. VOCKERAT.

Cross already? [*Holds him closer. Tenderly and earnestly.*] Think sometimes of God, my boy—even if it's only to please your old mother. That old Haeckel and that stupid Darwin, they do nothing but make you unhappy. Do you hear? Do it for your mother's sake.

JOHN.

[*Looks up despairingly.*] Good people, good people! you positively drive a man to the point of saying: Forgive them, for they know not . . . Do you really believe that it is such a simple matter—this turning pious?

MRS. VOCKERAT.

[*Moving away.*] Yes, Jack, yes! All that is needed is the will. Just try, Jack—only once. [*Exit on to verandah, where she seats herself and reads.*]

[JOHN *is once more absorbed in his manuscript.*

Enter KITTY *with letters.*

KITTY.

[*Reads, then looks up.*] John! here is a letter from the banker.

JOHN.

My dear Kitty, I really can't give my mind to such matters just now.

KITTY.

He asks if he is to sell out.

JOHN.

For goodness sake don't bother me about that at present!

KITTY.

But it must be attended to at once, John.

JOHN.

[*Angrily.*] Not at all! There—[*Taps nervously with his forefinger on the manuscript*] that is what must be attended to first!

KITTY.

Well, as you please. Only then we shall be without money to-morrow.

JOHN.

[*Still more violently.*] Upon my word, Kitty, we don't suit, you and I! You people are always wondering why a man can't settle down to work; but no sooner has he got his ideas into some little order, than there you come, bursting in, upsetting everything again.

KITTY.

I don't know what you mean. The post came and I told you—that was all.

JOHN.

Exactly—that was all. There you show your utter
want of any understanding. As if my work were like
shoe-making. The post comes and you tell me. Of
course! Why not? It never for a moment occurs
to you that by so doing you break a chain of thought
which it has taken no end of time and labour to link
together.

KITTY.

Still, practical matters must not be neglected.

JOHN.

But I tell you that my work comes first—first, and
second, and third! Then practical matters if you
choose! Do try to understand this, Kitty. Do try
to help me a little. If you like, keep every-day affairs
from me altogether. Take your own way in them.
Don't give me . . .

KITTY.

I should not like the responsibility, John.

JOHN.

There! You see! On no account any responsibility! On no account any independent action!
You women are simply determined to be dependent
—you do all that is in your power to remain irrespon-
sible agents.

KITTY.

[*Holds out the letter.*] Please, John, do say what is
to be done.

JOHN.

I tell you, Kitty, I can't think about it just now.

KITTY.

But when am I to come then, John? We can't speak about it before Miss Mahr.

JOHN.

There's another piece of narrow minded Philistinism —that keeping private of certain things—the making a mystery of everything connected with money matters. There's a sort of littleness about it that disgusts me.

KITTY.

I should like to see your face if I began to speak about these matters before Miss Mahr.

JOHN.

Why always Miss Mahr, Miss Mahr? Do let her alone. She is not in the way, is she?

KITTY.

I don't say that she is in the way. But it certainly can be of no interest to her to . . .

JOHN.

Kitty, Kitty! It's perfectly miserable, this constant talk and worry about money—as if we were on the verge of starvation. It's unendurable. It actually gives one the impression that your whole heart and mind are set on money, nothing but money. And I with my high ideal of woman. . . . What *is* a man to love?

KITTY.

It's not for myself at all that I care. But what is to become of our little Philip if . . . And you say yourself that you can't count on earning anything. Are we not bound, then, to take care of what we have?

JOHN.

Yes, yes, of course. It's simply this way; your
interests are limited by the family circle; mine are
wide, general ones. I am not the family man at all.
My one aim is to bring out what I feel lies latent in
me. I am like a yoked Pegasus. And it will be the
ruin of me some day.

KITTY.

John! You don't know how you hurt me by
saying such things.

JOHN.

Miss Anna is quite right. The kitchen and the
nursery bound the German married woman's horizon.
What lies beyond does not exist for her.

KITTY.

Some one must look after the food and attend to
the children. It's all very well for Miss Mahr to talk
like that! I should prefer to read books too.

JOHN.

If I were you, Kitty, I shouldn't show off' my own
littleness by speaking in such a way of a noble-minded
woman like Miss Anna.

KITTY.

If she can say such things . . .

JOHN.

What things?

KITTY.

About us German women—such stupid things.

JOHN.

She said nothing stupid. Far from that. 1 can
hardly bring myself to tell you at this moment how

she praised you.   I shouldn't like to make you feel ashamed.

KITTY.

All the same, she spoke about our narrow horizon.

JOHN.

Show that she is wrong, then!

KITTY.

[*In tears, passionately.*] John, John! good as you are, you are sometimes—sometimes so cruel, so cold, so heartless!

JOHN.

[*Somewhat cooled down.*] I am heartless again, am I? How do I show it, Kitty?

KITTY.

[*Sobs.*]   By   torturing   me.   You·· know—very well . . .

JOHN.

What do I know, Kitty?

KITTY.

You know—how dissatisfied I am with myself. You know it—but—but you have no compassion on me.   Every little thing is brought up against me.

JOHN.

What do you mean, Kitty?

KITTY.

Instead of—praising me a little sometimes—trying to give me a little confidence in myself—I am always made to feel—what a poor creature I am—always kept down.   God knows I don't pride myself on the wideness of my horizon.   But I have a little of some

sort of pride. I know well enough that I'm no
shining light. Indeed, I've long felt that I'm a
tolerably superfluous person.

JOHN.

[*Tries to take her hand,* KITTY *draws it away.*] You
are not superfluous, Kitty. I never said such a thing.

KITTY.

You said it a few minutes ago. But even if you
had not said it, I feel it myself—feel that I can be
nothing to you because I don't understand your work.
And as to little Philip—of course I can give him his
milk, and keep him clean . . . but a maid can do
that quite as well; and by-and-by—when he grows
up—I'll be no help to him either. [*Weeps more
passionately.*] He would be much better off with—
with Miss Anna.

JOHN.

You're never . . . my dear girl, how can you?

KITTY.

Of course I'm only joking, but yet it's true. She
has learned something. She knows and understands
things. We are helpless cripples. How can we be a
support to others, when we can't even . . .

JOHN.

[*Ardent and tender, tries to embrace* KITTY.] My
own Kitty! My sweet, sweet girl! You have a
heart of gold—a deep, rich, magic mine of treasure!
My darling! [*She pushes him away; he stammers.*] If
there is any honour in me I . . . I know I'm hard
and bad sometimes! I'm not worthy of you, Kitty!

KITTY.

No, no, John, please don't! You're only saying that just now because . . .

JOHN.

Because I mean it, Kitty. You may call me rogue if I . . .

KITTY.

Please let me alone, John! I must think.—And the letter—the letter!

JOHN.

You stupid Kitty, what is it you want to think about?

KITTY.

Many, many thoughts are rushing in on me. Stop, John! Let me go!

JOHN.

[*Eagerly.*] Oh, never mind the letter just now. My own sweet, sweet little wife!

KITTY.

No, John dear, no!   [*Holds him off.*

JOHN.

Why, Kitty, what's the matter with you?

KITTY.

You'll look at it, won't you, Jack? [*Holds out the letter.*] He asks if he is to sell out.

JOHN.

What shares?

KITTY.

The spinning-mill shares.

JOHN.

Can we not get along on the interest?

KITTY.

Quite impossible. This month again we have spent
more than a thousand marks.

JOHN.

Is it possible, Kitty? I can hardly believe it. Are
you good people economical enough?

KITTY.

You can see the accounts, John.

JOHN.

It's quite incomprehensible to me.

KITTY.

You give away too much, John. Then the capital
soon begins to go. Tell me, is he to sell these
shares?

JOHN.

Yes, of course. But there's no hurry! Anyhow,
it's of no consequence.—Where are you going?

KITTY.

To answer the letter.

JOHN.

Kitty!

KITTY.

[*At the door, turns round.*] Well, John?

JOHN.

Are you going away like that?

KITTY.

Like what?

JOHN.

I don't know either.

KITTY.

What is it you want?

JOHN.

I can't make you out, Kitty.   What's wrong?

KITTY.

Nothing at all, John.   Really.

JOHN.

Have you stopped caring for me?

[KITTY's *head droops*; *she shakes it depre-
catingly.*

JOHN.

[*Puts his arm round* KITTY.] Don't you remember
our promise, Kitty—that we were never to have
any secrets from each other?   Not even little ones.
[*Embraces her more warmly.*] Say something. Darling,
don't you care for me at all now?

KITTY.

O John! you know that I do.

JOHN.

What is it, then?

KITTY.

You know quite well.

JOHN.

I assure you I don't.   I have not the faintest idea.

KITTY.

It's only that I long to be something to you.

JOHN.

You are a great deal to me.

KITTY.

No, no!

JOHN.

But tell me . . .

KITTY.

You can't help it, John, but . . . I know that I don't satisfy you.

JOHN.

You do, Kitty. You are everything that I want.

KITTY.

So you say just now, John.

JOHN.

It is my most solemn conviction.

KITTY.

Yes, for the moment.

JOHN.

What can lead you to . . .

KITTY.

I see it plainly enough.

JOHN.

Kitty, have I ever given you cause . . .

KITTY.

No, never.

JOHN.

There, you see! [*Holds her closer to him.*] It is all

fancy—naughty fancies, Kitty, that must be driven away. Come, come! [*Kisses her tenderly.*

KITTY.

Oh, if it were only fancy!

JOHN.

You may be quite sure it is.

KITTY.

And—Jack dear—I do love you so!—Far more than any words can tell. I believe I could sooner give up baby than you.

JOHN.

Oh, Kitty!

KITTY.

It's a shame to say it!—The dear, sweet, funny little fellow! [*Her arms round* JOHN's *neck.*] My own dear, good husband!

[*Pause. Mute embrace.*]

[MISS MAHR, *dressed for going out, opens the verandah door.*

MISS MAHR.

[*Calls.*] I'm quite ready, Dr. Vockerat. Oh, I beg your pardon! [*Draws back.*

JOHN.

Immediately, Miss Mahr, immediately. [*Takes his manuscript.*] We're going for a row, Kitty.—No more fancies now, promise me! [*Kisses her, takes his hat, turns on his way out.*] Perhaps you would like to come too?

KITTY.

I can't go out just now, John.

JOHN.

Well, good-bye for a little !   [*Exit.*

[KITTY *gazes after him with the look of a
person watching the fading away of some
beautiful vision. Her eyes fill with tears.*

END OF THE SECOND ACT

THE THIRD ACT

[*Time: about* 10 *a.m.* KITTY *sits, absorbed in accounts, at the writing-table, on which a lamp is still burning.*

[*Scraping of shoes is heard outside the verandah door.* KITTY *looks up eagerly, and half rises. Enter* BRAUN.

KITTY.

[*Meets him.*] How kind of you to come, Mr. Braun !

BRAUN.

Good morning.   Isn't this fog horrible ?

KITTY.

It seems as if we were to have no daylight at all to-day. Come near the stove and get warm.—Did Mrs. Lehmann give you my message ?

BRAUN.

She did.

[KITTY *is no longer the same. She has exchanged her old quiet manner for a nervous liveliness. She is easily excited. Her eyes sometimes flash. There is a slight flush on her pale, emaciated cheeks.*

KITTY.

I'll get you a cigar.

BRAUN.

No, I can't allow that! [*Hurries after her, and himself gets down the box of cigars from the top of the bookcase.*]

KITTY.

Now do make yourself comfortable.

BRAUN.

[*Looks at* KITTY.] I don't like to smoke here.

KITTY.

You'll please me by doing it. I'm so fond of the smell.

BRAUN.

In that case . . .   [*Lights the cigar.*

KITTY.

You must make yourself at home, just as you used to do.—And now, you wicked person! what is the meaning of your not having come near us for a whole week?

BRAUN.

I thought Jack didn't need me.

KITTY.

But how could you . . . ?

BRAUN.

He has Miss Anna Mahr now.

KITTY.

How can you say such a thing?

BRAUN.

He said himself that his friends might go to Jericho.

KITTY.

You know his hasty way. That really meant nothing.

BRAUN.

I differ from you there. And I know very well whose influence we have to thank for this change. Miss Mahr may be a clever woman, but there is no doubt that she is a determined and egotistical one, unscrupulous in the pursuit of her aims. She is afraid of me. She knows quite well that she can't impose on me.

KITTY.

But what object could she have . . .

BRAUN.

Who knows what she may want with him? I don't suit her. I'm not the character to suit her.

KITTY.

But I have really never noticed . . .

BRAUN.

[*Rises.*] I thrust my company on no one. It was at Jack's request that I moved out here. If I am not wanted, I shall go back again.

KITTY.

[*Quickly and with peculiar emphasis.*] Anna leaves to-day.

BRAUN.

Indeed? She is going?

KITTY.

Yes. And that is why I wanted to ask you, Mr. Braun. . . . It would be so dreadful for John to be left suddenly without any one at all. You must begin and come regularly again, Mr. Braun. Don't bear him a grudge—I mean for these hasty words the other day. We know him. We know how warm-hearted he really is.

BRAUN.

I don't take offence easily, but . . .

KITTY.

That's all right, then, Mr. Braun. And now that you are here, you will stay and spend the day with us.

BRAUN.

I can't do that, but I might possibly come back later.

KITTY.

Try to be back, then, when Miss Anna leaves. You don't know how nice and cosy it's going to be here. I have had my eyes opened to many things. We are going to spend a very quiet, pleasant winter. —And by-the-bye, there was another thing I wanted to ask you. [*As if in joke.*] I must earn some money.— — Yes, yes, I mean it! Are we not intended to work too, we women?

BRAUN.

How have you suddenly taken this into your head?

KITTY.

It would be such fun, Mr. Braun.

BRAUN.

It's easy to talk about earning money.

KITTY.

Well, I can paint on china. I painted the dessert service. Or, if that is no good, I can embroider—on linen you know—beautiful initials and monograms.

BRAUN.

Of course you are only joking.

KITTY.

Don't be so sure of that!

BRAUN.

If you don't speak more clearly, I really can't . . .

KITTY.

[*Forgets herself.*] Can you keep a secret?—But no, no! The fact is—so many demands are made on people. . . . It isn't every one that has the gift of calculation.

BRAUN.

And Jack least of all.

KITTY.

Yes—no . . . that is—there is no good either in being too dreadfully exact. One must only make sure that there is enough.

BRAUN.

If you imagine that you can earn as much as that . . . I can tell you beforehand that it will be lost time and trouble.

KITTY.

But perhaps as much as twelve hundred marks a year.

BRAUN.

Twelve hundred marks! Hardly.—Why exactly twelve hundred?

KITTY.

I need that sum.

BRAUN.

Has Jack's boundless generosity been imposed on again?

KITTY.

No, certainly not.

BRAUN.

Then is it Miss Anna who is to be assisted?

KITTY.

No, no, no! What do you mean? How can you dream of such a thing? I'll say no more—not another word, Mr. Braun!

BRAUN.

[*Takes his hat.*] And I couldn't possibly aid and abet. It would really be . . .

KITTY.

Very well; then we'll say no more about it. But you'll come back?

BRAUN.

[*Ready to go.*] Of course, certainly.—Were you in earnest, Mrs. John?

KITTY.

[*Tries to laugh, but tears come into her eyes.*] No, no! I was joking. [*Motions him away eagerly, half playfully.*] Go away now, Mr. Braun, go! [*No longer able to master her emotion, rushes into the bedroom.*]   [*Exit* BRAUN, *thoughtfully.*

Enter MRS. VOCKERAT, *carrying a large dish
of apples. Seats herself at the table,
and begins to pare them.*

KITTY *returns, sits down at the writing-table.*

MRS. VOCKERAT.

[*Shakes the apples in the dish.*] It's a good thing
that we're going to settle down again, isn't it, Kitty?

KITTY.

[*Bending over her accounts.*] Don't speak to me,
please, mammy: I must think.

MRS. VOCKERAT.

I didn't notice.—I'll not disturb you.—Where is it
she is going?

KITTY.

To Zurich, I believe.

MRS. VOCKERAT.

Yes, yes. The right place for her too.

KITTY.

Why, mother, I thought you liked her.

MRS. VOCKERAT.

Not I; I don't care for her; she's too modern
for me.

KITTY.

Oh, mother!

MRS. VOCKERAT.

Nor do I think much of any young girl that can
go about for three days with a big hole in her
sleeve.

Enter JOHN *from the verandah, with his hat
on. Hurries towards the study.*

KITTY.

John !

JOHN.

Yes.

KITTY.

Shall I come to the station ?

JOHN.

[*Shrugs his shoulders.*] You ought to be the best
judge of that. [*Exit into study.*

[*Short pause.*]

MRS. VOCKERAT.

What's the matter with him now ? [*Has finished
paring the apples ; rises.*] Yes, it's high time things
were settling down again.—People are even beginning to talk.

KITTY.

About what ?

MRS. VOCKERAT.

I don't know. I only say . . . And besides it costs
money.

KITTY.

A fourth makes very little difference, mother, when
you are preparing food for three.

MRS. VOCKERAT.

That's all very fine, Kitty, but crumbs make
bread.

Re-enter JOHN. *He seats himself, crosses his
legs, and turns over the pages of a book.*

G

JOHN.

Impertinent wretches, these railway officials! A station-master who drinks, drinks, drinks all day long. And as insolent as . . . bah!

KITTY.

When does the best train go? Don't be annoyed, John!

JOHN.

Miserable hole! [*Slams the book noisily; jumps up.*] I won't stay here any longer.

MRS. VOCKERAT.

You have taken the house for four years, my boy.

JOHN.

And am I to go to the dogs here, simply because I have been unlucky and stupid enough to rent a house for four years?

MRS. VOCKERAT.

You were determined to come to the country, and you have hardly been here six months before everything is wrong again.

JOHN.

There's plenty of room for us in Switzerland.

MRS. VOCKERAT.

And baby? What's to become of him? Is he to be dragged all round the world too?

JOHN.

It will be healthier in Switzerland than here for him as well as for us.

MRS. VOCKERAT.

You will be off to the moon presently, my boy.

But you may please yourselves as far as I am concerned. An old woman like me doesn't expect to be taken into consideration at all. [*Exit by door to entrance-hall.*]

[*Short pause.*]

JOHN.

[*Sighs.*] I tell you, good people, you had better take care.

KITTY.

How do you come to think of Switzerland, John?

JOHN.

That's right; look as innocent as you can. [*Mimics her.*] " How do you come to think of Switzerland ? " I know that trick—underhandedness in place of straightforwardness. I know what you think. And you are quite right. I should like to be where Miss Anna is. There is nothing unnatural about that—nothing to prevent one saying it straight out.

KITTY.

John, you are so strange to-day. So strange . . . I had better go.

JOHN.

[*Quickly.*] I am going.   [*Exit by verandah.*

KITTY.

[*Sighs and shakes her head.*] Oh dear! Oh dear!

Enter MISS MAHR. *She lays hat, travelling-bag, and cloak in a chair.*

MISS MAHR.

I am quite ready. [*Turns to* KITTY.] Now we have still—how long?

KITTY.

Three quarters of an hour at least.

MISS MAHR.

Is that all ? I have been very happy here.
[*Takes* KITTY's *hand.*]

KITTY.

Time passes quickly.

MISS MAHR.

Now I'm going to bury myself in work at Zurich.
Work, work, and nothing else.

KITTY.

Let me get you something to eat.

MISS MAHR.

No, thank you ; I couldn't. [*Short pause.*] If only
the first meetings and visits were over ! Perfectly
horrible they'll be. Crowds of friends—endless ques-
tioning—birr ! [*Cold shiver.*] Will you write to me
sometimes ?

KITTY.

Oh yes ! but there is never much to tell.

MISS MAHR.

Will you give me your photograph ?

KITTY.

With pleasure. [*She searches in a drawer of the
writing-table.*] But it's an old one.

MISS MAHR.

[*Taps her gently on the back of the neck. Almost
pityingly.*] Thin little neck !

KITTY.

[*Still searching, turns her head. Smiles sadly.*] It has nothing weighty to carry, Anna. Here—this is it. [*Hands* ANNA *a photograph.*]

MISS MAHR.

Very nice, very nice! Do you think there is one of Dr. Vockerat too?—I have grown so fond of you all.

KITTY.

I don't know that there is.

MISS MAHR.

Look, Kitty, dear; please look! Have you one? —Yes?

KITTY.

Yes, there is one left.

MISS MAHR.

May I have it?

KITTY.

Yes, Anna, take it.

MISS MAHR.

[*Hurriedly slips the photograph into her pocket.*] And now—now I'll soon be forgotten by you all. O Kitty! O Kitty! [*Throws her arms round* KITTY's *neck and bursts into tears.*]

KITTY.

No, Anna, you won't. I'll always remember you, Anna; and . . .

MISS MAHR.

And care for me a little?

KITTY.

Yes, Anna, yes.

MISS MAHR.

Is it unmixed liking, Kitty?

KITTY.

I don't know what you mean by *unmixed*.

KITTY.

Are you not a little glad, too, that I am going away?

KITTY.

What ever do you mean, Anna?

MISS MAHR.

[*Has drawn away from* KITTY *again.*] Yes, yes, it's a good thing that I'm going, in every way. Mama Vockerat does not care for me any longer either.

KITTY.

I think you are mistaken in. . .

MISS MAHR.

No, Kitty, I'm not. [*Seats herself at the table.*] It's no use trying to persuade me. [*Forgets herself—takes the photograph from her pocket and gazes at it.*] There is such a deep line about the mouth.

KITTY.

Whose?

MISS MAHR.

John's. It's a line of unhappiness—loneliness brings it. A lonely person suffers much, has much to bear from others. . . . How did you get to know each other?

KITTY.

Oh, it was . . .

MISS MAHR.

He was still a student?

KITTY.

Yes, Anna.

MISS MAHR.

And you were very young, and you said Yes?

KITTY.

[*Red and confused.*] At least I . . .

MISS MAHR.

[*Feeling awkward too.*] Kitty, Kitty! [*She puts the photograph into her pocket. Rises.*] Must I be off now?

KITTY.

No, not for a long time yet.

MISS MAHR.

Long? Do you call that long? [*Seats herself at the piano.*] You don't play? [*KITTY shakes her head.*] Nor sing? [*KITTY again shakes her head.*] And John loves music, does he not?—I both played and sang— once. Not for many a day now. [*Jumps up.*] Never mind! What we have enjoyed we have enjoyed. We must not be greedy. There is a fragrance, a bloom, a glamour over these things, which is the best of them. Is that not so, Kitty?

KITTY.

I don't know.

MISS MAHR.

What smells so sweet is not always pure sweetness through and through.

KITTY.

That may be.

MISS MAHR.

I know it is. Oh! liberty!! liberty!!! The great thing is to be completely free—to have no country, no family, no friends.—Now it must be time.

KITTY,

Not yet, Anna.

[*Short pause.*]

MISS MAHR.

I get to Zurich too early—a whole week too early.

KITTP.

Indeed?

MISS MAHR.

If only work began at once! [*Suddenly throws her arms round* KITTY'*s neck; sobs.*] Oh, I am so miserably unhappy; so afraid of the future!

KITTY.

Poor, poor Anna!

MISS MAHR.

[*Hastily disengages herself from* KITTY'*s embrace.*] But I must go. I must.

[*Short pause.*]

KITTY.

Anna—before you go—won't you give me a little advice?

MISS MAHR.

[*Smiles sadly, almost compassionately.*] Dear Kitty!

KITTY.

You have the power to. . . . You have had such a good influence upon him.

MISS MAHR.

Have I ?   Have I really ?

KITTY.

Yes, Anna. And—and on me too. I owe you gratitude for many things. I have made a firm resolve. . . . Advise me, Anna.

MISS MAHR.

I can't advise you.   I am afraid to do it.

KITTY.

You are afraid ?

MISS MAHR.

I'm too fond of you, Kitty, much too fond.

KITTY.

If I could only do anything for you, Anna !

MISS MAHR.

You must not—you cannot.

KITTY.

Perhaps I can.   Perhaps I know what it is you are suffering.

MISS MAHR.

What am I suffering then, silly one ?

KITTY.

I would tell, but . . .

MISS MAHR.

Oh, nonsense, nonsense ! what should I be suffer-

ing? I came here and I'm going away again.
Nothing whatever has happened. Look, the <u>sun is</u>
actually shining again. We'll end up by taking a turn
round the garden. Whatever the circumstances,
hundreds and thousands are no better off. Or—by-
the-bye—I have a few words to write.

KITTY.

You can do that here. [*Makes room for her at the
writing-table.*] No, I see the ⬛ and pens are in
John's room. He is out. Go in there, Anna! [*She
opens the door for* ANNA, *remains behind herself.*]

[*Short pause.*]

Enter JOHN. *More restless than before.*

JOHN.

It's beginning to rain again. We should have
ordered a cab.

KITTY.

It is too late to do it now.

JOHN.

Yes, unfortunately.

KITTY.

Braun has been here.

JOHN.

That's a matter of tolerable indifference to me.
What did he want?

KITTY.

He intends to come again as usual, and things are
to be just as they were between you.

JOHN.

[*Gives a short laugh.*] Funny! That is supposed to

tempt me? . . . Could we not send yet—quickly?
Really, altogether . . .

KITTY.

For a cab, John? It's such a short way to the
station.

JOHN.

But the roads are in such a state, they're almost
impassable. It's altogether the most miserable
weather for travelling.

KITTY.

Once she gets into the train she will be all right.

JOHN.

Yes, in a crowded third-class carriage, with wet
feet.

KITTY.

She is sure to get into the ladies' compartment.

JOHN.

You might at least give her the big foot-warmer.

KITTY.

Yes, yes! you are right. I had thought of that
too.

JOHN.

Really—this is too miserable an ending up.

[KITTY *does not answer.*

JOHN.

I'm sure she would be glad to stay a few days
longer.

KITTY.

[*After a short pause.*] But you asked her.

JOHN.

[*More hastily.*] Yes, I did. But you did not—you and mother. You said nothing, and of course she noticed that.

KITTY.

O John! . . . No, no, I don't think so . . .

JOHN.

And with two people standing there—perfectly dumb—how can one go on insisting? It takes away one's very desire. . . . But I can't bear to be sending her away like this, in storm and darkness.

KITTY.

[*Goes up to him timidly and affectionately.*] No, no, John! Don't look at the thing in such a wrong light. And please don't always think so badly of me. It's not a question of sending away at all, John.

JOHN.

You and mother have not enough delicacy of feeling. You don't see. It seems to me as if we were simply showing her the door—nothing else. "You have been here long enough, you may go! Go wherever you like—away out into the wide world! Get on as best you can! Swim if you are able!" That is what it looks like to me, Kitty. We put ourselves to the trouble of expressing a little cold pity, that's all!

KITTY.

No, John! We have at least arranged matters so that she shall not suffer from want.

JOHN.

How do you know that she will accept it from us?

And even if she does—that's doing damned little for her. Money can't make up to her for want of friendliness.

KITTY.

But, John, she must go some time.

die Philister JOHN.

So Mrs. Grundy says, Kitty. She has been here, she has become our friend, and now Mrs. Grundy says it is time for us to part. It's a way of thinking that I don't understand. It's the sort of cursed nonsense that's always coming in one's way, destroying one's life.

KITTY.

Do you want her to stay, then, John?

JOHN.

I want nothing. I only say that it's a—that these principles of ours are nothing but the ordinary mean, narrow-minded worship of Mrs. Grundy. I can tell you that if it depended on me alone—if I were not tied and bound by all sorts of miserable little considerations—I should arrange these things very differently. I should set up a different standard of inward purity for myself, should have a cleaner conscience than I have now. You may be quite sure of that!

KITTY.

O John, John! I'm beginning to feel as if—as if you really didn't need me at all.

JOHN.

I don't know what you mean.

KITTY.

As if you were not contented with—with me alone.

JOHN.

Good God! Heaven preserve us!!! No—really—upon my word—this is the last straw! My nerves are not made of cast-iron. This is rather more than I can bear. [*Exit into garden.*

Enter MRS. VOCKERAT, *carrying a cup of beef-tea, which she puts down on the table.*

MRS. VOCKERAT.

There, that's for Miss Mahr.

KITTY.

[*With an outburst of despair runs to* MRS. VOCKERAT, *throws her arms round her neck, and sobs.*] Mother, mother! I must go—away from here—out of this house—away from you all. It's more than I can bear, mother, more than I can bear!

MRS. VOCKERAT.

Good gracious! My child, what's this? What ever . . . who has been . . .

KITTY.

[*Indignation taking the place of despair.*] No, I'm not such a poor creature as all that. I'll not allow myself to be set aside. I'm too good to be simply flung away. Mother, I must go this very moment. With the steamer—to America—away anywhere, only away—to England, where no one knows me, where . . .

MRS. VOCKERAT.

My good child!—to America! Goodness gracious!

are you mad? Are you going to leave your husband, to leave your child? Is little Philip to grow up without a mother? Never, never!

KITTY.

A pretty mother he has! A stupid, narrow-minded woman! What good can such a mother as I am be to him? Yes, I know how utterly stupid and narrow-minded I am. They have told me it every day. They have succeeded in making me out to be such a poor, miserable creature that I actually loathe myself. No, no! away, away!

MRS. VOCKERAT.

But, Kitty, you don't remember. . . . To leave husband and child . . . For God's sake think what it is you are doing!

KITTY.

Was he ever mine? First he belonged to his friends, now he belongs to Anna. He has never been satisfied with me alone. Oh that I had never been born! I am sick of life, accursed life!

MRS. VOCKERAT.

[*In her turn breaks forth excitedly, as if under the influence of a sudden enlightenment. Her set eyes sparkle, her colour changes.*] There, now! There, now! [*Points into vacancy.*] There! What did I tell you? What did I say? That a house from which God is banished is doomed to destruction. There you have it! Don't deceive yourselves. There! What did I say? First, deniers of God, then adulterers, then . . . Kitty!

KITTY.

[*Struggling against faintness.*] No, mother! No, no, mother! I . . . I . . .

MRS. VOCKERAT.

Kitty!—rouse yourself—come! I hear some one. Come! [*Exit with* KITTY *into bedroom.*

Enter JOHN *from the verandah.* MRS. VOCKERAT *opens the bedroom door.*

MRS. VOCKERAT.

Oh, it's you, John! [*Comes out, forcibly repressing her excessive emotion ; pretends to be looking for something.*]

MRS. VOCKERAT.

Well, my boy!

JOHN.

What, mother ?

MRS. VOCKERAT.

Nothing. [JOHN *looks at her questioningly.*] What is it, John ?

JOHN.

It seemed to me as if you . . . I must say that I don't like being watched.

MRS. VOCKERAT.

John, John! it's well for you that winter is coming. Your state is anything but . . . You never used to be so nasty to me. What you need is rest.

JOHN.

Yes, yes, of course! You all know better than I do what is good for me.

MRS. VOCKERAT.

And Kitty too, she is not at all so well yet as she ought to be.

JOHN.

Well, Anna has certainly not added much to her work.

MRS. VOCKERAT.

Perhaps not. But you must remember too that I am an old woman now—and however willing I may be, the old bones are apt to strike sometimes.

JOHN.

But there's no need for your working ; I have told you that a hundred times. There are plenty of servants in the house.

MRS. VOCKERAT.

Anyhow, it is time for Miss Mahr to be going back to her work again.

JOHN.

That is her affair.

MRS. VOCKERAT.

No, not altogether. There can be too much of a good thing. We have had enough of this   She has been here long enough.

JOHN.

What do you mean, mother, by speaking in this extraordinary way ? I can't understand . . .

MRS. VOCKERAT.

You want to ask Miss Mahr to stay on, and . . .

JOHN.

And I mean to do it, too. I shall most certainly

H

do it—most certainly. . . . Have you anything against it, mother?

MRS. VOCKERAT.

[*Warningly.*] My boy, my boy! . . .

JOHN.

No, mother! this is really . . . Any one would suppose I had committed a crime. It's more than . . .

MRS. VOCKERAT.

[*Affectionately persuasive.*] Now, my own boy, be reasonable! Do listen to me! Remember I'm your mother. It is for your good I'm speaking. No one would do more for you than I would. I know well how honourable you are—but we are weak creatures, John, the best of us . . . and Kitty is making herself miserable—and . . .

JOHN.

[*Laughs.*] Don't be offended, mother, but I can't help laughing. It's the only way to take it. It's perfectly ridiculous.

MRS. VOCKERAT.

John, John! stronger men than you have fallen into the snare. And before one knows it, it is often too late.

JOHN.

Mother! unless you people want to drive me out of my mind, you must not talk like this to me. Don't for God's sake confuse me, bewilder me, by suggesting things to me which . . . Don't drive me into positions which I never thought of; I implore you!

Mrs. Vockerat.

I suppose you know what you are doing, John. I only say to you—take care!

[*Exit* Mrs. Vockerat *into the bedroom.*

Re-enter Miss Mahr.

Miss Mahr.

[*Sees* John.] You are there, Dr. Vockerat! [*Takes her waterproof from the chair on which her things are lying, and proceeds to put it on.*] We must be going.

John.

[*Hastens to help her.*] Has it come to this?

Miss Mahr.

[*Fastening her cloak.*] What we were speaking about—you'll send me it soon?

John.

Yes, I'll not forget. But, Miss Anna, you might give me at least one little comfort. Will you not allow us the privilege of friends?

Miss Mahr.

You hurt me, Dr. Vockerat.

John.

Then I'll say no more about it. But you promise me—if you should ever be in a difficulty.—If others may help you, surely we may. [*Goes to the bedroom door and calls.*] Mother! Kitty!

Enter Mrs. Vockerat *and* Kitty.

Miss Mahr.

[*Kisses* Mrs. Vockerat's *hand.*] A thousand, thousand thanks! [Kitty *and* Anna *kiss each other affec-*

tionately.] My dear, kind Kitty!—and you'll remember
to write?

MRS. VOCKERAT.

I hope everything will go well with you, Miss
Anna.

KITTY.

Yes—and that you will be—[*she sobs*]—will be
happy. Don't . . . [*Can say no more.*]

[JOHN *takes* ANNA'S *bag.* KITTY *and* MRS.
VOCKERAT *accompany them on to the
verandah, where they meet* BRAUN, *who
takes leave of* ANNA. *General farewell.*
MRS. VOCKERAT, KITTY, *and* BRAUN
remain on the verandah, KITTY *waving
her handkerchief. Presently they re-
enter.*

MRS. VOCKERAT.

[*Comforting* KITTY, *who still weeps.*] Child, child!
comfort yourself! she'll get over it—she is young.

KITTY.

Those sad eyes of hers haunt me. Oh, she has
suffered much.

MRS. VOCKERAT.

Life is not a bed of roses for any of us, Kitty dear.

KITTY.

Oh, the misery of this weary world!
[*Exit into the bedroom.*

[*Short pause.*]

MRS. VOCKERAT.

She has not taken the beef-tea after all [*Lifts the
cup to carry it away, stops in front of* BRAUN.] Mr.

Braun, I can't help telling you that in these last ten minutes I have gone through more—yes . . . [*She takes a few steps towards the door, is suddenly overcome by weakness and obliged to sit down.*] It's taking effect on me now. I feel it in every limb. There's not a bit of strength left in in me.

BRAUN.

Has anything happened, Mrs. Vockerat?

MRS. VOCKERAT.

I'm not complaining. I'll not say one word if nothing worse comes of it than this. It has been a warning from our heavenly Father—and I—have understood it. . . . You are one of the godless too! Yes, yes! But you may take the word of an old experienced woman for it, Mr. Braun—we can't do without *Him*. Sooner or later we are sure to trip, and to fall. [*Short pause.*] I'm only—— [*She tries to rise, but is still too exhausted.*] Yes, I begin to feel it now. Who knows what harm it may have done me? [*Listens to sounds in entrance-hall.*] Who can that be? Is there not some one on the stair? Oh, I was forgetting—we are to wash to-morrow. The maids are fetching the linen to steep. There will be peace now to get something done. [*Short pause.*] Just see now—a man with such a character—an honourable, blameless man like John—just see what he is led into by trusting in his own strength. You say so grandly: Our religion is a religion of deeds. See what it comes to. God blows them down, these card houses of ours.

Enter JOHN *hurriedly from hall, excited, not very sure of himself.*

JOHN.

Good people, she has decided to stay.

MRS. VOCKERAT.

[*Not understanding.*] To stay, John !   How ?

JOHN.

Well, to stay a few days longer here, mother, of course.

MRS. VOCKERAT.

[*Stunned.*] Miss Anna has come . . . Where is she ?

JOHN.

She is in her room, mother.   I really don't understand . . .

MRS. VOCKERAT.

So you have done it after all ?

JOHN.

I must beg that you won't make such a dreadful fuss over things ; it . . .

MRS. VOCKERAT. -

[*Rises ; in a tone of command.*] John ! listen to me ! [*With emphasis.*] Miss Mahr's place is no longer here. I say to you plainly that she must leave the house again.   I insist upon it.

JOHN.

Mother, in whose house are we ?

MRS. VOCKERAT.

Oh, I have not forgotten.   I know only too well. We are in the house of a man who . . . who has forgotten what duty is . . . and, as you remind me of it . . . certainly, certainly !—I can make way for this, this person.

JOHN.

Mother, you speak of Miss Anna in a way that I cannot allow.

MRS. VOCKERAT.

And you speak to your mother in a way that is a transgression of the Fifth Commandment.

JOHN.

I'll control myself, mother. But I must ask you all to have some little consideration for my state of mind. I can't answer for myself if you don't. . . . If you drive me to it, I may do something which could not be undone again.

MRS. VOCKERAT.

A man that lays hands on himself is lost, for time and for eternity.

JOHN.

I can't help that. All the more reason why . . . why you should take care of what you are doing.

MRS. VOCKERAT.

I wash my hands of it all. I shall go.

JOHN.

Mother!

MRS. VOCKERAT.

Either this person leaves the house or I do.

JOHN.

Mother, you ask an impossibility. It was with the greatest trouble I persuaded her to change her mind. Am I to go to her now and . . . I'll rather shoot myself.

Mrs. Vockerat.

[*With sudden determination.*] Very well—then *I'll*
go. I'll tell her my opinion pretty plainly—the wily
coquette! the . . . She has entangled you nicely in
her net.

John.

[*Comes between* Mrs. Vockerat *and the door.*] You
shall not go near her, mother!! She is under my
protection, and I will not permit her to be insulted—
by any one.

Braun.

Jack, I say, Jack! . . .

Mrs. Vockerat.

I see now—my son—how far things have gone.
[*Exit by verandah door.*

Braun.

Jack, what in the name of goodness has happened
to you?

John.

Let me alone—you soul-destroyers!

Braun.

Don't be silly, Jack! You know me, Braun. I
have no intention of preaching to you.

John.

Your insinuations are degrading. It is moral com-
pulsion you are exercising. I am under torture. Not
another word do I say.

Braun.

No, no, Jack! This is not the time for silence.

As things stand now, you are bound to explain yourself. Try to be a little calmer.

JOHN.

What is it you all want to know? Of what are
we accused? No, my good friends, under no circumstances shall I try to prove my innocence to you. My
pride won't allow that, Braun. . . . Abominable . . .
the very idea of such a thing!

BRAUN.

Come now, Jack! I take a perfectly unbiassed
view of the situation.

JOHN.

Take any view of it you like. Only hold your
tongue about it, for every word you say is like a lash
in my face!

BRAUN.

You must confess, Jack, that you are playing with
fire.

JOHN.

I must confess nothing. It is not for you people
to pass judgment on my relations with Miss Anna.

BRAUN.

You can't deny, however, that you owe a certain
duty to your family.

JOHN.

And you can't deny that I owe a certain duty to
myself. Yes, Braun, you fellows boasted and bragged
—but now, when I take the first free step, you are
frightened, you begin to talk of duties, you . . .

BRAUN.

That was not what I meant at all. I know nothing

about duty! I only want you to see things as they are—to understand that it is a question of deciding between Anna and your family.

JOHN.

I really think you have gone off your head. Are you all determined to talk me into believing in a conflict of interests which does not exist? What you say is not true. There is no decision required. The bond between Anna and me is not the same as the bond between Kitty and me—there need be no clashing. It is friendship, damn it all! It is the result of a similarity of mind, combined with similar intellectual development, which enables us to understand each other, even when no one else understands us. She understands in me what you and my other friends cannot. Since she has been here I have been like a new man. Courage and self-esteem have come back to me. I feel creative power. And I feel that all this is her work—that she is necessary to my development. As friend, you understand. Is friendship between a man and a woman impossible?

BRAUN.

You must not be offended with me for saying it, Jack, but you have never been able to look things straight in the face.

JOHN.

It is you people who do not know what you are doing, I tell you. You judge by a miserable low standard, which I trample under foot. If you care for me at all, do not interfere with me. You don't know what is going on in me. That there may be danger now, after your attacks, is not at all impossible. But I have made up my mind to insure for myself, without transgressing bounds, what is to me a necessary of life. My mind is made up, you understand?

BRAUN.

This is your old mistake again, Jack. You are trying to reconcile things that are irreconcilable. As far as I can see, there is only one thing for you to do —go to her, tell her plainly how things stand, and ask her to leave.

JOHN.

Have you quite finished? Done at last? Well then, so that on this point at any rate there may be no misunderstanding, no further waste of words, I tell you —[*eyes flash ; emphasis laid on every word*]—*that I don't intend to do what you and mother want!!* I am not the man I was a short time ago, Braun. I am ruled by a different spirit; you and your opinion have lost all power over me. I have found myself, and intend to be myself—myself in spite of you all.

[*Exit quickly into the study.* BRAUN *shrugs his shoulders.*

END OF THE THIRD ACT

THE FOURTH ACT

Time, between 4 *and* 5 P.M. MRS. VOCKERAT *and* KITTY *are sitting at the table,* KITTY *sewing a baby's shirt,* MRS. VOCKERAT *knitting.* KITTY *looks terribly ill and emaciated. In the course of a few seconds, enter* JOHN *from the study, drawing on a summer overcoat, his hat only half on his head.*

JOHN.

Has Anna gone?

MRS. VOCKERAT.

[*Gives a sniff.*] Yes, this minute.

JOHN.

[*Goes up to* KITTY *and kisses her on the forehead.*] Are you sure you are taking your tonic regularly?

MRS. VOCKERAT.

Much good that stupid medicine will do her! I know what would be more to the purpose.

JOHN.

Now mother, mother!

MRS. VOCKERAT.

I'll say no more.

KITTY.

Yes, yes! I'm taking it. But I am really quite
well.

JOHN.

You certainly do look better to-day.

KITTY.

And I feel better too.

JOHN.

See you take good care of yourself, then. Good-
bye! We'll be back soon.

KITTY.

Are you going far?

JOHN.

Only into the wood a little. Good-bye!

[*Exit by verandah.*

[*Short pause. Rush and whistle of a railway
train are heard, then the distant sound of
the station bell.*

MRS. VOCKERAT.

Listen! there's the station bell.

KITTY.

Yes, the wind must be from that direction to-day,
mother. [*Drops her work and begins to dream.*

MRS. VOCKERAT.

[*Glancing at her.*] What are you thinking about,
Kitty dear?

KITTY.

[*Takes up her work again.*] Oh!—about a great
many things.

MRS. VOCKERAT.

What, for instance?

KITTY.

Well, I was wondering if there are people in the
world who have nothing to repent of.

MRS. VOCKERAT.

None, Kitty, you may be quite sure.

KITTY.

[*Holds out her work to her mother in-law.*] Should I
do chain-stitch here, mother? [*Shakes out the little
shirt.*] It's long enough, I think.

MRS. VOCKERAT.

Rather make it too long than too short.   Children
grow so fast.   [*Both work busily.*
             [*Short pause.*]

KITTY.

[*Continues to sew.*] John has sometimes had a great
deal to suffer—from my fancies. I have often felt
sorry for him.   But one cannot help one's nature—
that's the miserable thing. [*Gives a short bitter laugh.*]
I was too sure. I didn't know myself well enough.
[*Sighs.*] Sewing at this little shirt reminds me of an
old woman—a servant she was—in the institution at
Gnadenfrei, who had sewn her own shroud, and had
had it lying for years in her drawer. She showed it
to me once.   It made me quite melancholy.

MRS. VOCKERAT.

The silly old woman!

             [*Short pause.*]

KITTY.

[*Sewing.*] What a nice little boy that Harry Peters is! I brought him in yesterday and showed him some pictures. When we were looking at them he said: "The butterfly is the husband and the dragon-fly is the wife; that's the way, isn't it, Auntie Kitty?"

[MRS. VOCKERAT *laughs good-humouredly.*

KITTY.

Funny little fellow! And then he tapped me gently on the eyelids and asked, "Do the eyes sleep in there?"

MRS. VOCKERAT.

Children have sometimes pretty fancies.

KITTY.

[*With a touch of melancholy amusement.*] He still always says hankicher, instead of handkerchief, and then I tease him.

MRS. VOCKERAT.

Hankicher! [*Laughs.*

KITTY.

[*Lets the work drop into her lap.*] What sorrows children have too! I remember how for years when I was a child, I used to pray earnestly whenever I saw a potato-field, "O God, please let me find a big death's-head moth; only one!" But I never found it. [*She rises, fatigued. Sighs.*] When one grows up one has other disappointments.

MRS. VOCKERAT.

Where are you off to? Sit still a little longer.

KITTY.

I must see if baby is awake.

MRS. VOCKERAT.

Now don't fidget, Kitty! You know he'll be attended to.

KITTY.

[*Standing still, her hand to her forehead.*] Let me alone, mammy. I must think. *Towards John*

MRS. VOCKERAT.

[*Expostulates gently.*] That's exactly what you must not! Come—tell me something more. [*Draws her down on her chair, KITTY offering no resistance.*] There —sit down again. When John was a little boy he used to say very funny things too.

KITTY.

[*Sits as if in a dream, her wide-open eyes fixed on the portrait above the piano.*] Dear papa in his gown! He never dreamed what his daughter . . .
[*Her voice is choked by tears.*

MRS. VOCKERAT.

[*Notices.*] Kitty, Kitty dear!

KITTY.

[*Speaking with difficulty.*] Please, please don't speak to me.
[*Both work silently for a short time.*

KITTY.

[*Sewing.*] Were you very happy when John was born?

MRS. VOCKERAT.

I should rather think I was! Were you not happy about Philip?

KITTY.

I really don't know. [*Rises again.*] I really must go and lie down for a little.

MRS. VOCKERAT.

[*Also rises, strokes* KITTY's *hand.*] Yes, do, dear, if you don't feel well.

KITTY.

Take hold of my hand, mother.

MRS. VOCKERAT.

[*Does so.*] Why, it's as cold as ice, child!

KITTY.

Take the needle.   [*Holds it out to her.*

MRS. VOCKERAT.

[*Hesitates.*] What am I to do with it?

KITTY.

Look!
        [*Drives it quickly several times into the palm
            of her hand.*

MRS. VOCKERAT.

[*Seizes her hand.*] Good gracious, child! what are you doing?

KITTY.

[*Smiles.*] It doesn't hurt in the least. Not an atom. I feel nothing at all.

I

Mrs. Vockerat.

Silly fancies! Come, come! You had better lie down—much better.

[*Leads* Kitty *into the bedroom, supporting her a little.*

[*After a short pause, enter* Braun. *He takes off his hat and overcoat, and hangs them on the rack.*

Mrs. Vockerat.

[*Looks out at the bedroom door.*] Oh, it's you, Mr. Braun.

Braun.

Good morning, Mrs. Vockerat.

Mrs. Vockerat.

I'm coming this moment. [*Disappears; enters presently, hurries up to* Braun, *and puts a telegram into his hand.*] Advise me, Mr. Braun! [*Anxiously watches the expression of his face as he reads.*]

Braun.

[*Has finished reading.*] Have you told Mr. Vockerat how things are?

Mrs. Vockerat.

Indeed I have not! I couldn't bring myself to do it. I only wrote that I would like him to come, because . . . because I couldn't say how long I might have to stay, and because Kitty is not getting on so well as she ought to—nothing more, not even that Miss Anna is here yet.

Braun.

[*After a little reflection, shrugs his shoulders.*] Well, there is really nothing to be said.

MRS. VOCKERAT.

[*More anxiously.*] Do you think I was wrong?—
that it would have been better not to write? But
Kitty is fading away before my very eyes! If she
once takes to bed, then . . .ᵗI don't know what will be
the end of it. As it is, she has constantly to lie down.
She is lying down at this moment. I can't stand it
any longer, Mr. Braun. The responsibility is too
much for me to bear alone.   [*She wipes her eyes.*

BRAUN.

[*Looks at telegram.*] It is the six o'clock train that
Mr. Vockerat is coming by? What o'clock is it
now?

MRS. VOCKERAT.

Not half-past four yet.

BRAUN.

[*After a moment of reflection.*] Has there been no
change in the course of the week?

MRS. VOCKERAT.

[*Shakes her head hopelessly.*] None.

BRAUN.

Has she given no hint of any intention to go?

MRS. VOCKERAT.

Not the slightest. And as to John, he is perfectly
bewitched. He was always a little touchy and irritable, but in the end he generally did what one
wanted. Now he hears and sees no one but this
woman—mother and wife do not exist for him, Mr.
Braun. What in Heaven's name is to be done? I

lie awake all night.　I have thought it over in every possible way.　What is to be done?

[*Pause.*]

BRAUN.

I really don't know if it is a good thing that Mr. Vockerat is coming.　It will only serve to irritate John more, much more . . . And then . . . then he will feel obliged . . . I have sometimes the feeling that—that he would gradually work his way out of this if he were left alone.

MRS. VOCKERAT.

Just what I thought myself, Mr. Braun.　That was why I allowed myself to be over-persuaded when he brought her back again.　That was why I stayed on.　But no—things are getting worse and worse. One dare not so much as open one's mouth about it now.　I must not even mention the subject to Kitty. What am I to do?

BRAUN.

Has Mrs. John never spoken to her husband on the subject?

MRS. VOCKERAT.

Yes, once—they lay awake for half the night. God knows what passed between them.　But Kitty is far too patient.　She takes John's part whenever I say anything.　She does not even see through this . . . this . . . lady we are talking about.　She positively takes her part too.

[*Short pause.*]

BRAUN.

I have been wondering—if my speaking to Miss
Anna could possibly do any good.

MRS. VOCKERAT.

[*Quickly.*] I do believe it might.

BRAUN.

I once thought of writing to her . . . But seriously, Mrs. Vockerat, it seems to me that Mr.
Vockerat's interfering in the matter, in his way, may
make things very much worse.

MRS. VOCKERAT.

Oh dear! Oh dear! But where else was I to
turn in my distress? Oh, Mr. Braun . . . if you
would only speak to her! [ANNA's *and* JOHN'S *voices
are heard.*] No! I can't possibly meet her just now.
    [*Exit by door into entrance-hall.*
    [BRAUN *hesitates. As no one immediately
    appears, exit also by door into entrance-
    hall.*

Enter MISS MAHR *from the verandah.*

MISS MAHR.

[*Takes off her hat. Speaks through the open door to*
JOHN, *who has not come in from the verandah.*] Anything interesting going on, Doctor?

JOHN.

Something must have happened. There is a police-
man in the boat. [*Enter.*] Perhaps some one drowned
again.

MISS MAHR.

Why at once suppose the worst?

JOHN.

Such things happen here often enough. It is a dangerous little lake. What have you got there, Miss Anna ?

MISS MAHR.

Everlastings, Doctor Vockerat. I mean to take them with me as a remembrance.

JOHN.

Yes, when you go—which will not be for a long time yet.

MISS MAHR.

I'm not so sure about that.

[*Short pause, during which they walk up and down slowly, at differnt ends of the room.*

MISS MAHR.

It turns dark very early now.

JOHN.

And cold, as soon as the sun goes down. Shall I light the lamp ?

MISS MAHR.

As you like. Suppose we enjoy the twilight a little ? [*Seats herself.*

JOHN.

[*Also takes a chair, at some distance from* ANNA. *Pause.*] The twilight is the time for old memories, is it not ?

MISS MAHR.

And for fairy-tales.

JOHN.

Yes, for them too. And what beautiful ones there are !

MISS MAHR.

Yes. And you know how almost all the most
beautiful end?—I put on the glass slipper—and then
I tripped on a stone—there was a loud crack—and it
broke into bits.

JOHN.

[*After a short silence.*] Do you not call that sup-
posing the worst too?

MISS MAHR.

I don't think so. [*Rises, goes slowly to the piano,
sits down at it and rubs her hands.*]

JOHN.

[*Also rises, takes a few slow steps, and stands still
behind* ANNA.] Only a bar or two. Give me that
pleasure. I'll be quite satisfied with any simple little
air.

MISS MAHR.

I can't play.

JOHN.

[*In a tone of gentle reproach.*] Now, Miss Anna,
why say that? It's that you won't.

MISS MAHR.

For six years I had not touched a piano, until this
spring; then I made a beginning again; but I only
strum a little for my own pleasure—sad, hopeless
little songs, that I used to hear my mother sing.

JOHN.

Will you not sing me one of these sad, hopeless
little songs?

MISS MAHR.

There, you are making fun of me already.

JOHN.

I see you are determined not to oblige me, Miss
Anna.

[*Short pause.*]

MISS MAHR.

Yes, Dr. Vockerat, I am a horrid creature—full of
whims and fancies.

JOHN.

I didn't say that, Miss Anna.

[*Short pause.*]

MISS MAHR.

[*Opens the piano, lays her hands upon the keys.
Meditatively.*] If I only knew something lively.

> [JOHN *has seated himself in a far-off corner,
> with his legs crossed ; he rests his elbow on
> his knee and holds his hand to his ear.*]

MISS MAHR.

[*Lays her hands on her lap, speaks slowly and with
pauses.*] It is a great age that we live in.   That which
has so weighed upon people's minds and darkened
their lives seems to me to be gradually disappearing.
Do you not think so, Dr. Vockerat ?

JOHN.

[*Clears his throat.*] How do you mean ?

MISS MAHR.

On the one hand we were oppressed by a sense of
uncertainty, of apprehension, on the other by gloomy
fanaticism.   These exaggerated feelings are calming
down, yielding to the influence of something like a

current of fresh air, that is blowing in upon us from
—let us say from the twentieth century. Do you not
feel this too, Dr. Vockerat? People like Braun, for
instance, remind one of nothing so much as owls in
the daylight.

JOHN.

I don't know, Miss Anna! What you say about
Braun is true enough. But I don't find it possible to
arrive at any real joy in life yet. I don't know . . .

MISS MAHR.

It has no connection with our individual fates—our
little fates, Dr. Vockerat!

[*Pause.*]

[MISS MAHR *strikes a note and holds it
down.*

JOHN.

[*After the sound has died away.*] Well?

MISS MAHR.

Dr. Vockerat!

JOHN.

Please do play something!

MISS MAHR.

I have something to say to you—but you are not
to get angry; you are to be quite quiet and good.

JOHN.

What is it?

MISS MAHR.

I think my time has come. I want to go.

[JOHN *sighs deeply, rises and walks about
slowly.*

MISS MAHR.

Dr. Vockerat! we also are falling into the error of weak natures. We must look at things more impersonally. We must learn to take ourselves less seriously.

[*Short pause.*]

JOHN.

Must you really go ?

MISS MAHR.

[*Gently, but firmly.*] Yes, Dr. Vockerat.

JOHN.

I shall be ten times more lonely now than I was before.

[*Pause.*]

JOHN.

But we'll not talk about that at present.

MISS MAHR.

No. Only I must tell you that I have written to Zurich that they may expect me on Saturday or Sunday.

JOHN.

You have actually . . . but, Miss Anna, why this hurry ?

MISS MAHR.

There are many reasons.

[*Pause.*]

JOHN.

[*Walking about faster and more excitedly.*] And is one really to sacrifice everything that one has gained to this cursed conventionality ? Are people incapable

of understanding that there can be no crime in a
situation which only tends to make both parties better
and nobler? Do parents lose by their son becoming
a better, wiser man? Does a wife lose by the spiritual
growth of her husband?

MISS MAHR.

[*In a tone of gentle reproof.*] Dr. Vockerat! Dr.
Vockerat! think of the bad effect too.

JOHN.

[*More gently.*] But am I not right, Miss Anna?

MISS MAHR.

You are both right and wrong. . . . Your parents
see things in a different light from you. Kitty's view,
again, differs from theirs. It seems to me that in this
we cannot judge for them.

JOHN.

That is what is so dreadful—dreadful for us.

MISS MAHR.

For them . . . for the others no less so.

[*Pause.*]

JOHN.

Yes, but you have always said yourself that one
should not allow one's self to be ruled by the opinion
of others—that one ought to be independent?

MISS MAHR.

Unless one is dependent.

JOHN.

Granted. I am dependent—unfortunately! But
you? . . . Why do you take the others' part?

MISS MAHR.

~~Because~~ I have learned to love them too.

[*Pause.*]

MISS MAHR.

You have often said to me that you foresee a new, a nobler state of fellowship between man and woman.

JOHN.

[*Warmly, passionately.*] Yes, I feel that it will come some time—a relationship in which the human will preponderate over the animal tie. Animal will no longer be united to animal, but one human being to another. Friendship is the foundation on which this love will arise, beautiful, unchangeable, a miraculous structure. And I foresee more than this—something nobler, richer, freer still. [*Stops. Turns to* ANNA.] If it were not so dark I believe I should see you smiling. Am I right?

MISS MAHR.

No, Dr. Vockerat—I was not smiling this time, though it is true that such words—which are apt to carry away the speaker himself—do generally awake a spirit of ridicule in me. Let us suppose, however, that there may really have been something new, something nobler, in our relation to each other.

JOHN.

[*Suddenly.*] Can you doubt it? Shall I tell you how you may know it? Do you, for instance, feel anything for Kitty but the warmest affection? Is my love for her less strong than it was? On the contrary, it has grown deeper and fuller.

Miss Mahr.

But will you get any one, except me, to believe this? Will this prevent Kitty's grieving herself to death? . . . Don't let us speak of ourselves at all. Let us suppose, quite generally, the feeling of a new, more perfect relationship between two people to exist, as it were prophetically. It *is* only a feeling, a young and all too tender plant which must be carefully watched and guarded. Don't you think so, Dr. Vockerat? That this plant should come to perfection during our lifetime is not to be expected. We shall not see or taste of its fruits. But we may help to propagate it for future generations. I could imagine a person accepting this as a life-task.

John.

And hence you conclude that we must part.

Miss Mahr.

I did not mean to speak of ourselves. But it is as you say . . . we must part. Another idea . . . had sometimes suggested itself to me too . . . momentarily. But I could not entertain it now. I too have felt as it were the presentiment of better things. And since then the old aim seems to me too poor a one for us— too common, to tell the truth. It is like coming down from the mountain-top with its wide, free view, and feeling the narrowness, the nearness of everything in the valley. [*Pause.*

John.

But suppose it ruined no other life?

Miss Mahr.

That is an impossibility.

JOHN.

What if Kitty really possessed the power?—really succeeded in rising to the level of this idea?

MISS MAHR.

Even if Kitty were able—to live—sharing with me . . . I — I could not trust myself. There is something in me—in us—that opposes itself to these purer relations which we see dawning, Dr. Vockerat, something that in the long run would assert its power. Shall we have the lamp now?

Enter MRS. VOCKERAT *from the hall, with a light.*

MRS. VOCKERAT.

[*Calling back into entrance-hall.*] It's still dark here. Stay where you are for a moment, Mr. Braun, until I light the lamp. I'll arrange things so that . . .

[JOHN *coughs.*]

MRS. VOCKERAT.

[*Starting.*] Who is there?

JOHN.

We are here, mother.

MRS. VOCKERAT.

You, John?

JOHN.

Miss Anna and I, mother. Who is in the hall?

MRS. VOCKERAT.

[*Rather angrily.*] I must say, John, you might have lit the lamp. Sitting in the dark like this— really . . . [*Lights the lamp.* MISS MAHR *and* JOHN *sit still.*] John!

JOHN.

Yes, mother.

MRS. VOCKERAT.

Can you come with me for a minute? I want to speak to you.

JOHN.

Can't you do it here, mother?

MRS. VOCKERAT.

If you have no time to spare for me, then say so plainly.

JOHN.

Oh mother! of course I'll come. Excuse me, Miss Mahr. [*Exit with* MRS. VOCKERAT *into the study.*

MISS MAHR.

[*Begins softly striking simple chords, then sings to them in a low voice.*] " The tortures of prison sapped thy young strength ; to fate thy proud head bowing, with honour thou laid'st down thy life in thy loved people's cause." *

[*She stops.* BRAUN *has entered.*]

MISS MAHR.

[*Turns round on the piano-stool.*] Good evening, Mr. Braun.

BRAUN.

I did not mean to disturb you. Good evening, Miss Mahr.

MISS MAHR.

We have seen little of you lately, Mr. Braun.

BRAUN.

Oh! does it seem so?

* Words of a Russian Volkslied.

MISS MAHR.

I have heard the remark made several times.

BRAUN.

By whom? Not by John, I am sure.

MISS MAHR.

No, it was by Mrs. John.

BRAUN.

I knew it!—To tell the truth, I . . . But no, all that is of comparatively little importance now.

[*Pause.*]

MISS MAHR.

I think we are both in the humour to-day when it would do us good to hear something amusing. One must sometimes force one's self to laugh. Don't you know any entertaining stories, Mr. Braun?

BRAUN.

No, upon my word I don't.

MISS MAHR.

I don't believe you know what laughing means.

[*Pause.*]

BRAUN.

I really came, Miss Mahr, to talk to you—about something serious.

MISS MAHR.

You?—to me?

BRAUN.

Yes, Miss Anna.

MISS MAHR.

[*Rises.*] Go on, then, Mr. Braun. I am listening.

[*Goes to the table, unfastens the bunch of everlastings, and occupies herself arranging and re-arranging them.*]

BRAUN.

I was in the throes of a hard inward struggle—at the time I made your acquaintance—in Paris. It was an unnecessary one, for, after all, the question: Is one to paint with or without a serious motive? is most unimportant. Art is a luxury, and to be a luxury producer nowadays is a disgrace in any circumstances. At that time your influence was what helped me to my feet again. And, which is what I chiefly wanted to say, I learned at that time to respect and appreciate you.

MISS MAHR.

[*Busy with the flowers, flippantly.*] You don't express yourself with much delicacy, Mr. Braun—however, proceed.

BRAUN.

If such words as these offend you, Miss Mahr—then I regret . . . then I am quite perplexed.

MISS MAHR.

I am sorry for that, Mr. Braun.

BRAUN.

It is painful and disagreeable to me. One ought simply to let things take their course—if it were not for their serious consequences. But one can't . . .

MISS MAHR.

[*Humming the tune of "Spin, my daughter, spin away!"*] Pretty little everlastings.—I'm listening, Mr. Braun.

K

BRAUN.

When I see you like this, Miss Mahr, I can't help feeling that—that . . . You don't seem to be the least aware . . . you seem to have no idea whatever of the terribly serious state of matters.

[MISS MAHR *hums the tune of "Heiden-röslein.'*

BRAUN.

Yet every one has a conscience. There is nothing else for it, Miss Mahr—I must appeal to your conscience.

MISS MAHR.

[*After a short pause, coolly and flippantly.*] Do you know what Pope Leo the Tenth said about the conscience ?

BRAUN.

No, I do not, and at the present moment it is really a matter of indifference to me, Miss Mahr.

MISS MAHR.

He said it was a noxious animal which compelled men to take up arms against themselves.—But I beg your pardon ! I'm all attention.

BRAUN.

I don't know, but the thing seems to me so self-evident. You can't but see—that the very existence of a whole family is at stake. It seems to me as if one glance at young Mrs. Vockerat, one single glance, removed any possibility of doubt. I should have thought . . .

MISS MAHR.

[*Serious at last.*] Oh ! That is what we are coming to ! Well, go on, go on.

BRAUN.

Yes, and—and your—your relations with John.

MISS MAHR.

[*With a deprecating gesture.*] Mr. Braun!—It seemed to me that I owed it to the friend of my friend to listen to what he had to say—so far. Anything beyond this is spoken to deaf ears.

> [*Short embarrassed pause, after which* BRAUN *takes his hat and overcoat, and leaves the room with the air of a man who has done what he can.*

> [MISS MAHR *throws away her bouquet as soon as* BRAUN *has gone out, and walks up and down excitedly for a few seconds. She then becomes calmer and takes a drink of water.*

Enter MRS. VOCKERAT *from the hall.*

MRS. VOCKERAT.

[*Looks round anxiously, hastens towards* ANNA *as soon as she has made sure that there is no one else in the room.*] I am in such terrible anxiety—about my John. You know what a violent temper he has. There is something weighing on my mind. I can keep it back no longer, Miss Mahr. Oh, Miss Anna! Oh, Miss Anna!

> [*Looks at* ANNA *with a touching glance of entreaty.*

MISS MAHR.

I know what you want.

MRS. VOCKERAT.

Has Mr. Braun spoken to you?

[*Miss Mahr tries to say Yes, but her voice fails her. She bursts into a fit of weeping and sobbing.*

Mrs. Vockerat.

[*Trying to quiet her.*] Miss Anna! Dear Miss Anna! Don't let us lose our heads. Oh, what shall we do if John comes? What ever am I to do? Oh, Miss Anna, Miss Anna!

Miss Mahr.

It was only . . . I'm quite myself again. And you shall have no more cause for anxiety, Mrs. Vockerat.

Mrs. Vockerat.

I'm sorry for you too. I should be a cruel woman if I were not. You have had a hard life, and I feel truly for you. But yet John comes first with me—I can't help that. And you are very young yet, Miss Anna, very young. At your age people get over things more easily.

Miss Mahr.

It is inexpressibly painful to me that it should have come to this.

Mrs. Vockerat.

I never did such a thing before. I can't remember ever having been inhospitable. But I can't help myself. There is no other way out of it for us all.— I am not judging you, Miss Anna; I am speaking to you as one woman to another; I am speaking to you as a mother. [*Her voice is choked by tears.*] As my John's mother, I implore you to give him back to me! Give an unhappy mother back her child!

[*She has sunk down on a chair, and her tears fall on* ANNA's *hand.*]

MISS MAHR.

Dear, dear Mrs. VOCKERAT! This . . . this is terrible !——But—can I give back ? Is it true that I have taken anything?

MRS. VOCKERAT.

We won't enter into that. I don't want to examine into things, Miss Anna. I don't want to find out which tempted the other. I only know this, that never all his life has my son shown bad inclinations. I was so sure of him that—to this day I don't understand. . . . [*She weeps.*] It was presumption on my part, Miss Anna.

MISS MAHR.

You may say what you please, Mrs. Vockerat, for I can't defend myself. . .

MRS. VOCKERAT.

I don't want to hurt you. I wouldn't for the world anger you. For I am in your power. All I can do in my anguish of heart is to beg you, to implore you to let John go—before it is too late—before Kitty's heart is broken. Have pity !

MISS MAHR.

Mrs. Vockerat ! You make me feel myself too utterly vile. . . . I feel as if I were being beaten ; and . . . But no—I'll say nothing except that I was already prepared to go. And if that is all . . .

MRS. VOCKERAT.

I don't know what you'll think, Miss Anna. I can hardly bring myself to say it. But because of certain

circumstances . . . it would need to be at once . . .
within an hour you must if possible . . .

> [MISS MAHR *collects the outdoor things which
> she had taken off.*

MRS. VOCKERAT.

Necessity compels me, Miss Anna.

> [*Short pause.*]

MISS MAHR.

[*Her things over her arm, walks slowly in the direction of the door into entrance-hall; she stops in front
of* MRS. VOCKERAT.] Could you suppose that I would
still delay ?

MRS. VOCKERAT.

God be with you, Miss Anna !

MISS MAHR.

Good-bye, Mrs. Vockerat !

MRS. VOCKERAT.

Shall you tell John what has passed between us ?

MISS MAHR.

You need have no anxiety about that, Mrs.
Vockerat.

MRS. VOCKERAT.

God bless you, Miss Anna.

> [*Exit* MISS MAHR *by door into entrance-hall.*
> MRS. VOCKERAT *draws a long breath of
> relief, and hurries off into the bedroom.
> A lantern appears on the verandah. Enter*
> OLD VOCKERAT *in travelling cloak and
> cap, followed by a station porter loaded
> with packages.*

VOCKERAT.

[*Beaming with satisfaction.*] What! No one here?
Lay the things on the table. Wait a minute! [*Looks
in his purse.*] Here's something for your trouble.

PORTER.

Thank you, sir.

VOCKERAT.

Stop, my good friend. [*Looks in the pockets of his
cloak,*] I thought—I was sure I had a few left—
" Palm Leaves " . . . Here they are! [*Hands him
one or two little paper books.*] He was a true Christian
who wrote these. Actual experiences. May they be
blessed to you! [*He shakes hands with the bewildered
PORTER, who, not knowing what to say, retires silently.*

[VOCKERAT *hangs up his cloak and cap, looks
about, rubs his hands cheerfully, and
then goes and listens at the bedroom door.
Hearing some one approach it, he runs
and hides behind the stove.*

KITTY.

[*Entering from bedroom, sees the parcels, cloak, and
cap.*] What! Surely these are—surely these are—
these are papa's things.

VOCKERAT.

[*Rushes out from behind the stove, laughing and
crying at the same time quite uncontrollably. He
embraces KITTY, and kisses her repeatedly.*] My
daughter! My little Kitty! [*Kiss.*] How are you
all? What's going on? Are you all well and in
good spirits? [*Kiss.*] You've not the least idea . . .
[*Lets KITTY go*] not the very least idea how I have
looked forward to this day. [*Laughing all the time.*]

And what's our prince about?—ha, ha, ha! How is
his highness, ha, ha! Our little Prince Sniffkins, ha,
ha, ha, ha! Thank God that I'm here again at last!
[*Rather exhausted.*] Do you know—[*taking off his
spectacles and rubbing the glasses*]—it's all very well to
live alone for a short time, but it doesn't do in the
long run. Ha, ha! Man does not thrive on a lonely
life; he's happier far when he takes a wife. Ha, ha,
ha, ha! Yes, yes, that's the way of it! And then,
you know, it was a very busy time, too—dung carting,
you know. Dung, ha, ha, ha! that's the farmer's
gold. When Pastor Peters came to see me lately, he
found fault with me for having the dung-heap so near
the house. [*Laughs.*] But I said to him : "My good
sir, do you not know," said I, "that this is our gold-
mine?" Ha, ha, ha, ha! But where's my old lady
all this time—and where's John? [*Looks more closely
at* KITTY.] I don't know—can it be the lamp-light?
It strikes me that you are not looking so well yet as
you used to do, Kitty.

KITTY.

[*With difficulty concealing her emotion.*] Oh, yes,
papa dear, I feel quite . . . [*Throws her arms round
his neck.*] I'm so glad you have come!

VOCKERAT.

I surely didn't . . . yes, I did give you a fright,
Kitty. What a shame of me!

>   [MRS. VOCKERAT *appears at the entrance-hall
>   door.*

VOCKERAT.

[*Much excited again.*] Hurrah! Ha, ha, ha, ha!

Here she comes! [*He and his wife rush into each other's arms, weeping and laughing.*]

[*Exit* KITTY, *quite overcome.*

VOCKERAT.

[*After their silent embrace, clapping his wife on the back.*] Well, well, my dear old woman!—We were never away from each other so long before.—Now we only want John.

MRS. VOCKERAT.

[*After a short hesitation.*] Our visitor is here still.

VOCKERAT.

A visitor, do you say?,

MRS. VOCKERAT.

Yes, the young lady.

VOCKERAT.

What young lady?

MRS. VOCKERAT.

Why, you know! Miss Mahr.

VOCKERAT.

I thought she had gone. But look here, I've brought plenty of provisions with me. [*He turns over the packages.*] Here is butter. I brought no eggs this time, remembering what disasters we had with the last. This is cheese—for John—home-made. These things must be taken to the cellar at once. Here's a ham—and it's a delicately-cured one too, I can tell you, Martha—like salmon.—But you're so quiet. You're well, I hope?

MRS VOCKERAT.

Yes, yes, papa. But—but I have something on my mind. I first thought I wouldn't tell you about it—but—I . . . You are my own dear husband. I can bear it no longer. Our son . . . our John—has been on the brink . . .

VOCKERAT.

[*Looks astonished, then alarmed.*] What! John? Our boy John? What is it? Tell me at once.

MRS. VOCKERAT.

Yes, but you are not to be alarmed. Thanks be to God, the danger is over. At least—the lady is leaving the house this evening.

VOCKERAT.

[*Painfully affected.*] Martha! This *cannot* be true.

MRS. VOCKERAT.

I have no idea how—how far they have gone—but . . . oh, what I have endured !

VOCKERAT.

I would have staked my right hand on his honour, Martha, without one moment's hesitation.—*My* son —Martha! my son — to forget his duty and his honour!

MRS. VOCKERAT.

Don't take it so to heart, yet. You must investigate into the matter. I don't even know . . .

VOCKERAT.

[*Walks about, pale, murmuring to himself.*] Thy will be done ! Thy will be done !

[MRS. VOCRERAT *sheds tears silently.*

VOCKERAT.

[*Stopping in front of her ; in a hollow voice.*] Martha
—we are being punished.—Let us search our hearts.

MRS. VOCKERAT.

We have looked on in silence and allowed our
children to stray farther and farther from God and
the right way.

VOCKERAT.

Just so. That is it. And now we are being
punished. [*Takes his wife by both hands.*] But we
will humble ourselves in prayer to God, Martha—day
and night, day and night.

END OF THE FOURTH ACT

THE FIFTH ACT

*The action follows almost directly on that of Act IV.
No one in the room. The lamp is still burning
on the table.*

Enter JOHN *hurriedly from the hall.*

JOHN

[*Angrily.*] Mother! [*Opens the bedroom door.*]
Mother!

Enter MRS. VOCKERAT *from bedroom.*

MRS. VOCKERAT.

Well, John, what's the matter? What a noise
you're making! You'll waken baby.

JOHN.

I should like to know, mother, who gave you the
right to—to turn visitors out of my house.

MRS. VOCKERAT.

O John! . . . I never dreamt of doing such a
thing. I have turned no one out of the house.

JOHN.

[*Walking furiously up and down.*] You lie,
mother!!

MRS. VOCKERAT.

You are not ashamed to use such language to your
mother ?   John, John !

JOHN.

I can't help it.   It is the case.   Miss Anna is
going, and . . .

MRS. VOCKERAT.

Did she tell you that I was driving her away?

JOHN.

She didn't need to tell me.   I know it.

MRS. VOCKERAT.

How can you possibly know that, my boy ?

JOHN.

She is going.   You have worked and worked to
bring it about.   But I tell you this—she'll go over
my dead body.   You see this revolver?   [*Takes one
out of the bookcase.*]   I put it to my head—so, and
if she goes out of this house I draw the trigger.   I
solemnly swear it.

MRS. VOCKERAT.

[*Terrified, tries to catch hold of his arm.*] John !
. . . for goodness' sake, don't !   Don't do that !

JOHN.

I give you my word . . .

MRS. VOCKERAT.

[*Calls.*] Papa ! papa ! come here !   How easily it
might go off and . . . Papa ! come and make him
listen to reason.

Enter VOCKERAT *from the bedroom.*

JOHN.

F—ather ! [*Suddenly comes to himself, lowers the revolver.*]

VOCKERAT.

Yes, here I am——and is this—this the way you meet me ?

JOHN.

What does it all mean, mother ?

VOCKERAT.

[*Going towards him slowly and solemnly.*] That you must think what you are about, my son—that is what it means.

JOHN.

What has brought you here just now ?

VOCKERAT.

The will of God, boy. Yes, God's will has brought me here.

JOHN.

Did mother send for you ?

VOCKERAT.

Yes, John.

JOHN.

For what purpose ?

VOCKERAT.

To help you, my boy, as your true friend.

JOHN.

Why should I need help ?

VOCKERAT.

Because you are weak, John—a poor, weak creature like the rest of us.

JOHN.

And suppose I am, what will you do to help me?

VOCKERAT.

[*Goes up to him, takes his hand.*] First I will tell you how much we all love you—yes! And then I will tell you that God rejoices over a sinner, yes, over a sinner who repents.

JOHN.

And so I am a sinner?

VOCKERAT.

[*Still gently.*] A great sinner, yes—in the sight of God.

JOHN.

In what does my sin consist?

VOCKERAT.

He that looks on a woman to lust after her, says Christ, yes—and you have done more—yes, yes!

JOHN.

[*Holds his hands to his ears.*] Father . . .

VOCKERAT.

Nay, John, don't close your ears! Give me your hand—sinner to fellow-sinner—and let me fight the battle with you.

JOHN.

I must tell you, father, that we take our stand on quite different ground.

VOCKERAT.

The ground you stand on is crumbling beneath your feet.

JOHN.

How can you say that, father? You don't know
on what ground I stand. You don't know what path
I take.

VOCKERAT.

I do. The broad path that leads to destruction.
I have silently looked on, yes—and so has a higher
than I—God. And because I knew that, I neglected
what was my duty, yes! But to-day I come in His
name, and say to you, Turn! you are on the edge of
a precipice.

JOHN.

Good words and kindly meant, father . . . but I
must tell you that they find no echo in my breast. I
am not afraid of your precipices. But there are
other precipices—beware of driving me over their
brink!

VOCKERAT.

No, no, John! . . . no . . .

JOHN.

It is not true that whoever looks at a woman to
desire her commits adultery. I have struggled and
struggled . . .

VOCKERAT.

No, John, no! I have often given you advice
before, which you have proved to be good. I say to
you to-day, Don't deceive yourself—put an end to
it! Think of your wife, of your boy, and think a
little too of your old father and mother. Don't
heap . . .

JOHN.

Am I not to think of myself at all, father?

VOCKERAT.

As soon as you have made up your mind, you will feel free and happy.

JOHN.

And if I don't ?

VOCKERAT.

Take my word for it, you will.

JOHN.

And if . . . and Miss Anna ?

VOCKERAT.

The worldly-minded, John, get over such things easily.

JOHN.

But what if she does not ?

VOCKERAT.

Then it has not been God's will.

JOHN.

Well, father, I differ from you. We don't under-stand each other. In this matter I don't suppose we ever shall.

VOCKERAT.

[*Struggling to maintain a friendly tone.*] It's—it's not a question of understanding. You mistake the position—yes, yes! That's not the position in which we stand to each other at all, as you used to know very well. It's no question of coming to an understanding.

JOHN.

Excuse me, father, then what is it a question of ?

VOCKERAT.

Of obeying, it seems to me.

L

JOHN.

You think that I should do what you wish, even if it seems wrong to me?

VOCKERAT.

You may be sure that I'll not advise you to do anything wrong. I'm sorry that it should be necessary to say this to you . . . to remind you . . . how we brought you up—not without toil and trouble and many a sleepless night. We nursed you when you were ill, John, never sparing ourselves; and you were often ill, my boy, yes! And we did it all willingly, gladly.

JOHN.

Yes, father, and I am grateful to you for it.

VOCKERAT.

So you say, but these are words, and I want to see deeds, deeds. Be a good, a moral man, and an obedient son—that is real gratitude.

JOHN.

So you consider me ungrateful; I don't reward you for your trouble?

VOCKERAT.

Do you remember the prayer you used to say when you were a little child, every morning, yes, and evening, in bed?

JOHN.

Well, father?

VOCKERAT.

"O God, I humbly pray to Thee
That I Thy faithful child may be;
And if I from Thy paths do stray . . .

JOHN.

"Then take me, Lord, from earth away." So you think it would have been better if I had died?

VOCKERAT.

If you continue to wander on the downward path, if . . . .yes!—if you go on hardening your heart.

JOHN.

I almost think myself that it would have been better.

[*Short pause.*]

VOCKERAT.

Be yourself again, my son. Think of your old teachers, John—think of Pastor Peters and all his pious admonitions. Imagine . . .

JOHN.

[*Frantic.*] Father, stop these reminiscences, unless you want to make me laugh. Reminding me of my teachers, indeed!—a pack of blockheads who educated the marrow out of my bones!

MRS. VOCKERAT.

Gracious heavens!

VOCKERAT.

Quiet, Martha, quiet! [*To* JOHN.] Neither your teachers nor your parents have deserved this of you.

JOHN.

[*Screams.*] They were my destruction

VOCKERAT.

This is blasphemy, John.

JOHN.

I know what I am saying. You have been my
destruction.

VOCKERAT.

Is this the reward of our love?

JOHN.

Your love has been my destruction.

VOCKERAT.

I don't recognise you, John—I can't understand
you.

JOHN.

You are right there, father. None of you ever
did or ever will understand me.

[Short pause.]

VOCKERAT.

Very well, John! I'll say no more. I did not
think things had gone so far. I hoped to be able to
help you, but that hope is at an end. Only God can
help you now. Come, my poor old Martha; we have
nothing more to do here. We'll go and hide our
heads somewhere until it pleases God to take us. [*He
turns again to* JOHN.] But, John, one thing more I
must say to you: keep your hands free from blood.
Do you hear?—free from blood! Do not bring that
too upon yourself.—Have you ever noticed Kitty
lately? Do you know that we are in fear of her
mind giving way? Have you ever really looked at
the poor, sweet young creature, eh? Have you the
least idea of what you have done to her? Get mother
to tell you how she sobs and cries at night over your
old photographs. Once more then, John, beware of

blood-guiltiness !—Now we are ready to go—yes, yes
Come, Martha, come !

JOHN.

[*After a short struggle.*] Father !! Mother !!
  [VOCKERAT *and his wife turn round.* JOHN
    throws himself into their arms.

VOCKERAT.

O John !

[*Pause.*]

JOHN.

[*In a low voice.*] Tell me what to do.

VOCKERAT.

Don't keep her. Let her go, John.

JOHN.

I promise you that I will.

[*Sinks exhaustedly on to a chair.*
  [MRS. VOCKERAT, *overcome with joyful emo-
    tion, hurries into the bedroom.*

VOCKERAT.

[*Claps* JOHN *gently on the back, kisses his forehead.*]
Now God give you strength—yes, yes !

[*Exit into bedroom.*
  [JOHN *sits quiet for a moment; then, he
    shudders, rises, looks out at the window
    into the darkness, opens door into entrance-
    hall.*

JOHN.

Is any one there ?

MISS MAHR.

Yes, Dr. Vockerat, I am.   [*Enters.*

JOHN

Were you going without saying good-bye ?

[*Walks up and down.*

MISS MAHR.

I half thought of doing so.   But it doesn't matter now.

JOHN.

My situation is a terrible one.   Father is here.   I have never seen him in such a state.   The blithe, jovial man !   I can't get over it.   And yet how am I to sit still and see you go, Miss Anna, and . . .

MISS MAHR.

You know, Dr. Vockerat, that I should have had to go anyhow.

JOHN.

No, you are not to go !   You must not !   Most certainly not now—at this moment.

[*Is seated again, holding his hand to his head, groaning deeply.*

MISS MAHR.

[*In a voice hardly audible from emotion.*]   Dr. Vockerat !   [*Lays her hand gently on his head.*

JOHN.

[*Raises his head ; sighs.*]   O Miss Anna !

MISS MAHR.

Remember what we said to each other hardly an hour ago.—Let us make a virtue of necessity.

JOHN.

[*Rises and walks about excitedly.*]   I don't know

what we said. My brain is racked, confused, vacant.
I don't know what I said to father. I don't know
anything! My brain is an ugly blank.

Miss Mahr.

Dear Dr. Vockerat, if only our last minutes together might be clear, conscious ones!

John.

[*After a short struggle.*] Help me, Miss Anna!
There is no manliness, no pride left in me. I am
quite changed. At this moment I am not even the
man I was before you came to us. The one feeling
left in me is disgust and weariness of life. Everything has lost its worth to me, is soiled, polluted,
desecrated, dragged through the mire. When I
think what you, your presence, your words made me,
I feel that if I cannot be that again, then—then all
the rest no longer means anything to me. I draw a
line through it all and—*close my account.*

[*He walks about, stops in front of* Anna.

Give me something to hold on by. Give me something to cling to—a support. I am falling. Help
me! I am on the verge of destruction, Miss Anna!

Miss Mahr.

It grieves me terribly, Dr. Vockerat, to see you
like this. I hardly know how I am to help you.
But one thing you ought to remember—that we fore-
saw this. We knew that we must be prepared for it
sooner or later.

[John *stands still, reflecting.*]

Miss Mahr.

Now you remember, don't you? Shall we try it?

—you know what I mean. Shall we make a law for ourselves—and act according to it all our lives, even if we never see each other again—our own one law, binding us two alone? Shall we? There is nothing else that can unite us. Don't let us deceive ourselves. Everything else separates us. Shall we do this? Are you willing?

JOHN.

I do feel—that this might support me. I might be able to work on, hopeless of attaining my aim. But who is to answer for me? Where am I to draw my faith from? Who is to assure me that I am not wearing myself out for nothing at all?

MISS MAHR.

If we will a thing, Dr. Vockerat, what need is there of faith, of guarantees?

JOHN.

But if my will is not strong?

MISS MAHR.

When I feel mine weak, I shall think of him who is bound by the same law, and I know that that will give me strength. I shall think of you, Dr. Vockerat!

JOHN.

Miss Anna—— Well, then, *I will! I will!*— Our prophetic feeling of a new, a free existence, a far-off state of blessedness—that feeling we will keep. It shall never be forgotten, though it may never be realised. It shall be my guiding light; when this light is extinguished, my life will be extinguished too. [*Both silent and overcome.*] I thank you, Miss Anna!

Miss Mahr.

Good-bye, John!

John.

Where shall you go?

Miss Mahr.

I may go north—I may go south.

John.

Will you not tell me where?

Miss Mahr.

Don't you think it is better that you should not ask?

John.

But shall we not from time to time . . . let each other know . . . only a few words to tell where we are, what we are doing . . .

Miss Mahr.

[*Shakes her head, smiling sadly.*] Would that be wise? Does not the greatest danger of failure lie that way?—in our yielding to ourselves? And failure would mean that we have been deceiving our-selves.

John.

Be it so, then—I will bear the burden. I will clasp it tight—even if it should crush me. [*Has taken* Anna's *hand.*] Good-bye.

Miss Mahr.

[*Speaking with difficulty, sometimes timidly, changing colour, showing strong emotion throughout.*] John! one word more! This ring—was taken from the finger of a dead woman, who—who had followed her

—her husband . . . to Siberia—and faithfully shared his sufferings—to the end. [*With a little mocking laugh.*] Just the opposite to our case.

JOHN.

Miss Anna!

[*He lifts her hand to his lips and holds it there.*

MISS MAHR.

It is the only ring I have ever worn. Its story is a thing to think of when one feels weak. And when you look at it—in hours of weakness—then—think too of her—who, far away—lonely like yourself—is fighting the same secret fight.—Good-bye!

JOHN.

[*Wildly.*] *Never, never* to meet again!

MISS MAHR.

If we meet again we are lost.

JOHN.

But how am I to bear it?

MISS MAHR.

What does not overcome us strengthens us.

[*Turns to go.*

JOHN.

Anna!   Sister!

MISS MAHR.

[*In tears.*] My brother!

JOHN.

May not a brother—kiss his sister—before they part for ever?

Miss Mahr.
No, John.

John.
Yes, Anna!   Yes, yes!

[*He takes her into his arms, and their lips
meet in one long, passionate kiss.   Then
Anna tears herself away, and goes out by
the verandah.   John stands for a moment as
if dazed, then strides up and down, putting
his hand through his hair ; sighs, sighs
again more deeply, stands still and listens.
The noise of the approaching train rushing
through the wood is heard.   John opens
the verandah door, and stands listening
there.   The sound grows louder, and then
gradually dies away.   The station bell is
heard.   It rings a second time—a third
time.   Shrill whistle of the departing train.
John turns to go into his room, but breaks
down on the way ; sinks on to a chair, his
body shaken by a convulsion of weeping
and sobbing.   Faint moonlight on the
verandah.*

[*Voices are heard in the bedroom.   John
jumps up, goes towards the study, stops,
thinks for an instant, and then hurries
out by the verandah.*

*Enter Vockerat from the bedroom, followed by his wife.
Both go towards door into entrance-hall.*

Vockerat.
[*Stopping.*] John!—I thought I heard some one
here.

MRS. VOCKERAT.

[*At door into entrance-hall.*] Some one has just gone upstairs.

VOCKERAT.

Yes, yes! What he wants now is rest. We'll not disturb him. What would you say, though, to sending Braun up to him?

MRS. VOCKERAT.

The very thing, papa! Minna shall go for Mr. Braun. I don't know, though, if I shouldn't go to John myself.

VOCKERAT.

[*Going towards verandah door.*] Better not, Martha. [*He opens the door; listens.*] Beautiful clear moonlight. Listen!

MRS. VOCKERAT.

[*Comes quickly from entrance-hall door.*] What is it?

VOCKERAT.

Wild geese—look! there! over the lake. The black specks you see crossing the moon.

MRS. VOCKERAT.

No, old man, my eyes are not so young as they once were.   [*Goes back to entrance-hall door.*

VOCKERAT.

Listen, Martha!

MRS. VOCKERAT.

What is it now, papa?

VOCKERAT.

[*Shuts the door and follows his wife.*] Nothing! I

only thought I heard some one moving about down there—fumbling with the oars.

MRS. VOCKERAT.

Who should be doing that at this hour?

[*Exit both by door into entrance-hall.*
[*Some one is seen peering through the verandah window. It is* JOHN. *He presently enters, stealthily. He is changed in appearance, is deathly pale, and breathes open-mouthed. Glances round hurriedly, afraid of being discovered. Gets writing materials and writes a few words; jumps up, throws down the pen, and hurries out by the verandah as soon as sounds are heard.*

Re-enter MR. *and* MRS. VOCKERAT, *with* KITTY *between them.*

MRS. VOCKERAT.

Did any one ever hear of such a thing? Sitting alone in the pitch-dark!

KITTY.

[*Holding her hand before her eyes.*] The light dazzles me.

MRS. VOCKERAT.

What a naughty, naughty girl! In the dark for who knows how long?

KITTY.

[*Half suspiciously.*] What? . . . Why are you both so good to me?

VOCKERAT.

Because you are our own, only, dear daughter.

[*He kisses her.*

KITTY.

[*Smiling faintly.*] Yes, yes! You are sorry for me.

MRS. VOCKERAT.

There's nothing else wrong, is there, Kitty?

VOCKERAT.

Let's say no more about it, Martha. Things will be all right again now. The worst is over, thank God.

KITTY.

[*Sitting at the table; after a short pause.*] Mother, I feel. . . . The light is still dazzling me. . . . I feel like a person who has been attempting to do something perfectly foolish, but who has come to her senses again.

MRS. VOCKERAT.

How so, dearie?

KITTY.

Has Anna gone, mother?

VOCKERAT.

Yes, Kitty. And now—now you must be happy and bright again.

[KITTY *remains silent.*]

MRS. VOCKERAT.

Don't you love John any longer, Kitty?

KITTY.

[*After thinking a little.*] I have not been so badly off, after all. My friend Fanny Stenzel married a pastor. But however contented and happy she may

be, do you think I would change with her? Not I.
—There's a smell of smoke here, isn't there?

MRS. VOCKERAT.

No, child, I smell nothing.

KITTY.

[*Wringing her hands piteously.*] Oh dear! Oh dear!
Things can never come right again—never!

VOCKERAT.

You must have more faith, my dear daughter.
Mine has come back to me, and my sure trust that
all will be well. God has sometimes strange ways of
leading erring souls back to Himself. I believe,
Kitty, that I can trace the workings of His purpose.

KITTY.

The first feeling that I had, mother, when John
came and asked me to marry him, was the right one.
I remember how all that day the thought was never
out of my head: What can such a clever, learned man
want with a creature like you? What can you be to
him? And you see, I thought rightly.

MRS. VOCKERAT.

No, Kitty, no! The truth is that it is not you
who need to look up to John, but John who needs to
look up to you; you stand high above him.

VOCKERAT.

[*With a trembling voice.*] But . . . what Martha
says is true, yes, yes! but—if you can forgive . . .
if you can forgive his great sin . . .

KITTY.

Oh, if there were only anything to forgive! I could forgive once—a hundred times—a thousand times. But John . . . John is not a man to do anything disgraceful. A poor creature like me has nothing to forgive John. It all comes from my being what I am and not something else. I know now exactly what I am and what I am not.

[*Repeated cries of* " Hallo there !" *are heard outside.*

MRS. VOCKERAT.

I'll tell you what we'll do, Kitty. I'll help you to get to bed, and then sit beside you and read aloud to you—"Grimm's Fairy Tales"—until you fall asleep. And to-morrow morning early you shall have a little nice hot soup and a soft-boiled egg, and then you will get up, and we'll go into the garden, and the sun will be shining bright, and everything will seem quite different. Come !

Enter BRAUN *from verandah.*

BRAUN.

Good evening !

VOCKERAT.

Good evening, Mr. Braun !

BRAUN.

How do you do, Mr. Vockerat ? [*Shakes hands with him.*] Is John here ?

VOCKERAT.

He is upstairs, I think.

BRAUN.

Is he ?—are you sure ?

VOCKERAT.

I believe so. Isn't he, Martha? What makes you
doubt it, Mr. Braun?

BRAUN.

I'll just look and see.

[*Exit quickly by door into entrance-hall.*

MRS. VOCKERAT.

[*Rather anxiously.*] What does Mr. Braun mean?

KITTY.

[*Excitedly.*] Where is John?

MRS. VOCKERAT.

Don't you be anxious, Kitty. He can't be far off.

KITTY.

[*With rapidly-increasing anxiety.*] But where is
he?

VOCKERAT.

Upstairs—upstairs, of course.

[*Re-enter* BRAUN. *Momentary pause of
anxious expectation.*

VOCKERAT.

Well, Mr. Braun?——

BRAUN.

No, he's not upstairs, Mr. Vockerat, and . . .
and . . .

VOCKERAT.

Well, what's the matter?

BRAUN.

Nothing, nothing!

M

KITTY.

[*Rushing up to* BRAUN.] Yes, there is something !

BRAUN.

No, really ! There's really no cause for anxiety—
only—I have the feeling that John ought not on any
account to be left alone at present. And just now as
I was—oh ! it's probably all nonsense.

MRS. VOCKERAT

What is it, Mr. Braun ? do say.

VOCKERAT.

Speak out, man ; don't lose time.

BRAUN.

When I opened the garden gate, I heard some one
unchaining a boat, and as I came round some one
rowed out. I don't know who it was—a man—and
it flashed into my mind—but he gave no answer.
And John would have answered.

KITTY.

[*Frantically.*] It was John ! it was John Run,
run, for God's sake run ! Mother ! Father ! It is
you who have driven him to this. Why did you do
it ? . . .

MRS. VOCKERAT.

O Kitty !

KITTY.

I feel it. He is unable to live any longer. I'll do
anything he likes, gladly. But O God, not this ! not
this !

VOCKERAT.

[*Hurrying down the garden, calls at intervals.*]
John ! John !

KITTY.

[*To* BRAUN.] A man ? And you called ? Did he
not answer ? Oh, run !

[*Exit* BRAUN.

KITTY.

[*Calls after him.*] I'm coming too. [*Wrings her
hands.*] O God ! if he is only alive and can hear me !

[BRAUN *is heard down at the lake, calling*
" Hallo, there ! hallo ! "

KITTY.

[*Opening door into entrance-hall, calls.*] Alma !
Minna ! Bring lanterns into the garden. Lanterns
—quick !

[*In the act of hurrying out on to the verandah
she sees the note, stands stock-still, then
goes forward, stiff and quivering, lifts it,
stares at it for a few seconds as if stunned,
and falls to the ground. Continued calling
outside.*

CURTAIN

Printed by BALLANTYNE, HANSON & Co
London & Edinburgh

CPSIA information can be obtained
at www.ICGtesting.com
Printed in the USA
LVOW04s1605310316

481609LV00022B/924/P